Social Mobility and Political Change

Key Concepts in Political Science
GENERAL EDITOR: Leonard B. Schapiro
EXECUTIVE EDITOR: Peter Calvert

Other titles in the same series include:

ALREADY PUBLISHED
Martin Albrow   **Bureaucracy**

IN PREPARATION

Shlomo Avinieri	**Utopianism**
Stanley Benn	**Power**
Anthony H. Birch	**Representation**
Peter Calvert	**Revolution**
Brian Chapman	**Police State**
Karl Deutsch	**Legitimacy**
S. E. Finer	**Dictatorship**
Joseph Frankel	**National Interest**
C. J. Friedrich	**Tradition and Authority**
Julius Gould	**Violence**
Eugene Kamenka and Alice Erh-Soon Tay	**Law**
J. F. Lively	**Democracy**
Robert Orr	**Liberty**
P. H. Partridge	**Consent and Consensus**
John Plamenatz	**Ideology**
John C. Rees	**Equality**
Bernard Schaffer	**Modernization**
Leonard B. Schapiro	**Totalitarianism**
Henry Tudor	**Political Myth**

Social Mobility and Political Change

Ioan Davies
University of Essex

Praeger Publishers
New York · Washington · London

Praeger Publishers, Inc.
111 Fourth Avenue, New York, N.Y. 10003, U.S.A.
5 Cromwell Place, London sw7, England
Published in the United States of America in 1970
by Praeger Publishers, Inc.
Library of Congress Catalog Card Number: 75-95669
Printed in Great Britain

Contents

'Key Concepts'
an Introductory Note

Political concepts are part of our daily speech—we abuse 'bureaucracy' and praise 'democracy', welcome or recoil from 'revolution'. Emotive words such as 'equality', 'dictatorship', 'élite' or even 'power' can often, by the very passions which they raise, obscure a proper understanding of the sense in which they are, or should be, or should not be, or have been used. Confucius regarded the 'rectification of names' as the first task of government. 'If names are not correct, language will not be in accordance with the truth of things', and this in time would lead to the end of justice, to anarchy and to war. One could with some truth point out that the attempts hitherto by governments to enforce their own quaint meanings on words have not been conspicuous for their success in the advancement of justice. 'Rectification of names' there must certainly be: but most of us would prefer such rectification to take place in the free debate of the university, in the competitive arena of the pages of the book or journal.

Analysis of commonly used political terms, their reassessment or their 'rectification', is, of course, normal activity in the political science departments of our universities. The idea of this series was indeed born in the course of discussion between a few university teachers of political science, of whom Professor S. E. Finer of Manchester University was one. It occurred to us that a series of short books, discussing the 'Key Concepts' in political science would serve two purposes. In universities these books could provide the kind of brief political texts which might be of assistance to students in gaining a fuller understanding of the terms which they were constantly using. But we also hoped that outside the universities there exists a reading public which has the time, the curiosity and the inclination to pause to reflect on some of those words and ideas which are so often taken for granted. Perhaps even 'that insidious and crafty animal', as Adam Smith described the politician and statesman, will occasionally derive some pleasure or even profit from that more leisurely analysis which academic study can afford, and which a busy life in the practice of politics often denies.

It has been very far from the minds of those who have been concerned in planning and bringing into being the 'Key Concepts' series to try and impose (as if that were possible!) any uniform pattern on the authors who have contributed, or will contribute, to it. I, for one, hope that each author will, in his own individual manner, seek and find the best way of helping us to a fuller understanding of the concept which he has chosen to analyse. But whatever form the individual exposition may take, there are, I believe, three aspects of illumination which we can confidently expect from each volume in this series. First, we can look for some examination of the history of the concept, and of its evolution against a changing social and political background. I believe, as many do who are concerned with the study of political science, that it is primarily in history that the explanation must be sought for many of the perplexing problems of political analysis and judgement which beset us today. Second, there is the semantic aspect. To look in depth at a 'key concept' necessarily entails a study of the name which attached itself to it; of the different ways in which, and the different purposes for which, the name was used; of the way in which in the course of history the same name was applied to several concepts, or several names were applied to one and the same concept; and, indeed, of the changes which the same concept, or what appears to be the same concept, has undergone in the course of time. This analysis will usually require a searching examination of the relevant literature in order to assess the present stage of scholarship in each particular field. And thirdly, I hope that the reader of each volume in this series will be able to decide for himself what the proper and valid use should be of a familiar term in politics, and will gain, as it were, from each volume a sharper and better-tempered tool of political analysis.

There are many today who would disagree with Bismarck's view that politics can never be an exact science. I express no opinion on this much debated question. But all of us who are students of politics—and our numbers both inside and outside the universities continue to grow—will be the better for knowing what precisely we mean when we use a common political term.

London School of Economics and Political Science

Leonard B. Schapiro
General Editor

Preface and Acknowledgements

The case for the consideration of social mobility as a concept used by political scientists rests on the obvious fact, noted by most commentators during the nineteenth century, that many of the political upheavals which characterized Western Europe and North America from the end of the eighteenth century were associated with changing patterns of social mobility. Since then, however, sociologists have paid much attention to social mobility, but not to its relationship with political change, while political scientists concerned with change have paid some attention to social stratification but not, on the whole, to mobility. This book is therefore to a large extent an attempt to return to some of the basic preoccupations of earlier political scientists while at the same time examining the accumulated knowledge and research which has unfortunately been affected by the division of the topic between two disciplines. There is considerable writing on the relationship between class, status and other stratification features and politics, but on the whole this has lacked the historical and dynamic emphasis which interested John Stuart Mill, de Tocqueville, Weber and Durkheim. Ultimately the importance of social stratification for the political scientist is not that societies have different measurements and dimensions of social inequality but that these forms of stratification are constantly changing. The important issue is whether changes in political structure necessarily affect social differences and vice versa.

By its very nature, such a study must be comparative, in time and across societies. As far as possible this book tries to base its account on as much comparative material as possible. Inevitably there are gaps. Asia is hardly treated at all, most of the historical evidence is ignored and the use of data in relation to particular theories is often random and purely illustrative. But to have been systematic and detailed as well as comparative would have required a much longer book. I can only hope that my suggestions of the importance and dimensions of the topic will stimulate the reader to examine this other material in greater detail.

I am pleased to make certain acknowledgements. The major part of Chapter 4 appeared in the *Socialist Register 1967*. (I must thank the editors, Ralph Miliband and John Saville, as well as the publishers, Merlin Press, for permission to reproduce material.) Shakuntala de Miranda helped with some of the basic research; she was a model of what an academic colleague should be. Many undergraduate and post-graduate students at the University of Essex read sections of the manuscript and commented. If there are any virtues in the book they come from the fact that it was written as part of a teaching programme. If there are any failings they show that the teacher was not as good as his students.

Colchester,   Ioan Davies
November, 1969

1/Political Theory and Social Mobility

Sociological studies of politics often seem to be concerned exclusively with the problem of social class. This approach is no Marxist monopoly. From Aristotle to Adam Ferguson and Disraeli a concern with the distribution of power by indices of social difference was one of the main preoccupations of philosophers and political scientists. In the *Politics* Aristotle based much of his analysis of stable and unstable societies on the distribution of social groups in relation to the power structure[1] and defined types of political system by the social class in control: e.g. an oligarchy was government by the rich and democracy was government by the poor. Much subsequent political analysis has explored the relationship between social structures and political power and, like Aristotle, has used 'ideal types' of policy in an attempt to analyse comparative political structures. Marx's contribution was primarily to have activated the classification by arguing in favour of the powerless classes and by basing his theory of politics squarely on conceptions of class struggle. Class, for Marx, was not a static concept but closely related to economic and social change.

Thus the concern of this book is not with class as such: it can be argued that static class situations are of relatively little interest to sociologists concerned with political change. The major interest in class is in its relationship to shifts in the distribution of power and the nature and scope of institutional control. For example, our interest in Manchu China is not simply in the distribution of its social classes but in the way that the political system controlled or anticipated shifts in this social structure. Likewise the decline in the Chinese empire and the rise of nationalism raised questions about the viability of the political system but often the questions referred to the empire's changing social structure. The fact that relationships between dominant groups are changing must be considered when explaining political changes.

In modern industrial society the changes are dramatic enough to pose questions about the entire scale of values that affect relationships between political structures and populations. It is hardly surprising that writers in Britain and France at the beginning of the nineteenth century saw social mobility and the values associated with it as a central issue in explaining industrialization, revolution and reform of political structures. Edmund Burke argued that 'modern life' is characterized by the fact that 'human beings are no longer born to their place in life . . . but are free to employ their facilities . . . to achieve the lot which may appear to them most desirable'.[2] Concern with the *values* accompanying mobility as well as the actual rates of changes in social stratification is displayed by writers from de Tocqueville and Adam Smith to such contemporary authors as Lipset and Ossowski.

This book is therefore less about 'normal' situations of stability than about periods of active political change. Its emphasis is not on the large number of variables relevant to the study of political change but on the somewhat narrower consideration of how shifts in the composition, orientation and distribution of social groups have a bearing on what is sometimes described as the 'political system'. The importance of the subject is well suggested by Pitrim A. Sorokin in his study of social mobility first published in 1927: 'During these years circulation in the political field has been going on with an extraordinary rapidity and over the widest range. The political aristocracy has been recruited from the lowest classes and the classes themselves, at least temporarily, have changed their relative position in the whole social pyramid.[3]

On a different level, that of the relationship between political attitudes and mobile groups, the same issue arose in Britain in 1959 after the Labour Party had lost its third successive general election. Abrams and Rose[4] conducted a survey to establish why people were not voting Labour and concluded that a significant percentage of traditional Labour voters were failing to identify with the party because of increased affluence. The more consumer goods they bought the more likely they were to identify with the middle class and move from a party which they saw as the representative of the deprived. Although most subsequent research has shown this to be based on false premises,[5] the issue is critical. To what extent does a shift in class position—either in terms of the acquisition or loss of facilities or values within a class or by actual changes in the system of stratification—include a change in the political orientation of the members of the class and in the responses of the political system?

This latter point is as crucial as the first. Taking the case of the Labour Party in 1959 it might be argued that Labour's electoral success in 1964 and 1966 disproved Abram's and Rose's thesis. On the other hand it might equally be argued (with some justification) that by the middle of the 1960s the Labour Party had changed its public image in response to the attitudes of this 'new' working class and had done this successfully enough to gain its support. The problem is therefore two-fold: to identify social mobility and to suggest its impact on the political system.

In this chapter and the next we shall examine the development of the analysis of mobility in its political context by outlining the origins of modern social theories. Subsequently we shall examine some of the situations the theories try to explain in an effort to assess the pertinence of different levels of explanation.

The classical theories

The classical theories of mobility and political change originate in the late nineteenth century although their case material is derived from many earlier periods as well as from the European industrial revolutions. But their major preoccupations were the transformations accompanying the French Revolution, the American War of Independence and the English industrial revolution.

For most theorists there were five central issues in the transition to industrial society: the shift from a community-based society to one founded on association (that is from organic, rural communities to voluntaristic, urban relationships); the shift from traditional, ascriptive authority to rational, legally-based power; the replacement of sacramental religious motivations by secular ones; the growing alienation of men in industrial and urban situations; and the reorganization of social stratification from ascriptive, hierarchical pyramids to structures based on economic incentive, consumer behaviour and political status. In each of these the study of social mobility and political change was central, for what exercised all theorists—political, sociological and philosophical—was the decline of old social groups and the emergence of new ones.[6]

De Tocqueville speaks for them all when he remarks: 'As the classes that managed local affairs have been suddenly swept away by the storm, and as the confused mass that remains has neither yet the organisation nor the habits which fit it to assume the administration of these affairs, the state alone seems capable of taking upon itself all the details of government, and centralization becomes, as it were, the unavoidable state of the country.'[7]

Here we have some of the essential ingredients of nineteenth-century social analysis: old classes disappeared, new ones emerged, and the political system had changed, producing a more centralized structure of power. As with the other writers to be considered, de Tocqueville measured the changes against previous situations (in his case a typology of aristocratic order) while at the same time attempting to predict what future structures were likely to arise. He argued that the industrial revolution in England had produced new lower classes who wanted power centralized in order to protect themselves against the localized authority of the upper classes. In time, however, the position would be reversed: it would be the lower classes who sought local autonomy and the upper classes who would insist on centralization. The nineteenth century was transitional. The upper classes were still fighting political campaigns in favour of the older, aristocratic decentralization but ultimately they would fight for the new power base of a centralized society. De Tocqueville commented wryly: 'I confess that I put no trust in the spirit of freedom which appears to animate my contemporaries. I see well enough that the nations of this age are turbulent, but I do not clearly perceive that they are liberal; and I fear lest, at the close of these perturbations which rock the base of thrones, the dominions of sovereigns may prove more powerful than ever it was'.[8] The increase in social mobility and the consequent fluidity in social structures would inevitably lead to less individual freedom and a more rigid centralization of power. The values associated with increased mobility not only raised questions about the composition and circulation of political élites but also about the whole foundation of political organization. In America social differences were less marked than in aristocratic societies; mobility was more frequent and accepted as a social norm. Because of this, 'society at large is naturally stronger and more active, individuals more subordinate and weak'.[9] To achieve a measure of freedom, individuals and groups would have to accept the centralized contours of the new society and build from there.

As one of the most perceptive analysts of the political consequences of mobility, de Tocqueville based his observations on the cultural processes of the three societies he knew well—England, France and America—but his approach to political analysis was descriptive and intuitive, contrasting with many of the sociologists who wrote in the nineteenth and early twentieth centuries. If he was concerned with the loss of freedom in industrial democracies, not all other theorists were as strongly influenced by 'possessive individualism'.[10] His reference point was the freedom of the aristocracy ('among aristocratic nations the mass is often sacrificed to the individual and the prosperity of the greater number to the greatness of the few') and if equality and social flux meant centralization they also implied less freedom for the aristocracy.

Marx's emphasis was distinctly different. He believed that the crux of the issue in the transition to industrial society was not the rise of the democracies but the change in the mode of production. The centralizing trends which de Tocqueville noted were not a consequence of egalitarianism. The shifting methods of production and capital accumulation 'employ the power of the state, the concentrated and organised force of society, to hasten, hot-house fashion, the process of the transformation of the feudal mode of production into the capitalist mode'.[11] Industrial civil society is thus in a large part a result of changing methods of production. Egalitarianism is possessive individualism: 'the basis of the modern state is civil society and the individual of civil society, that is the independent individual whose only link with other individuals is private interest and unconscious natural necessity, the slave of wage labour, of the selfish needs of himself and others'.[12] The problem of social mobility and egalitarianism is therefore directly related to the division of labour produced by capitalism. Its importance is not in its intrinsic characteristics but in the way it blinds the mobile to the real contradictions of capitalism. 'The size of one's purse is a purely quantitative difference by which two individuals of the same class may be brought into conflict.'[13]

The real issues in class differences are therefore, for Marx, not those of income but of productive relations. In all societies there are three great classes; the landed gentry, the capitalists and the proletariat. If mobility into the gentry class is unlikely, into the capitalist class it is only possible by acquisition of capital. Otherwise a form of mobility may occur within the proletariat, but it is more likely to be downward mobility: 'the lower strata of the middle class—the small tradespeople, shopkeepers, and retired tradesmen generally, the handicraftsmen and peasants—all these sink gradually into the proletariat, partly because their diminutive capital does not suffice for the scale on which modern industry is carried on, and is swamped in the competition with the large companies, partly because their specialized skill is rendered worthless by new methods of production'.[14] On the other hand the use of machinery creates new wealth and requires a new class, dependent on the capitalists, to consume the new luxuries while at the same time reducing the numbers of productively employed workers and replacing them with servants and service workers. The problem then is not social mobility as such, but on the one hand the productive relationships and on the other the ideologies and social consciousness of workers and capitalists. Mobility in terms of shifts in jobs from less menial to more specialized, or in increases in income, is only a modification or consequence of the relation of worker to production.

The political implications of these socio-economic processes are clear enough. Within the ruling class there will be conflicts between the landed gentry and the capitalists, and even between different kinds of capitalists on such technical details as the pace of mechanization or reallocation of land. The arrival of newly mobile groups such as the Free Traders of mid-nineteenth-century England initiates a struggle for power between different sections of the ruling class. This process is the central feature of political change and again is rooted in changes in production. The feudal lords give way to the merchants, the merchants to industrial capitalists. In time the capitalists too will give way to a powerful, unified working class based on the new means of production. The whole of political history is based on group mobility, which is itself the result of far-reaching changes in the economy.

Meanwhile the capitalist ruling class maintains its control partly through the machinery of state and economic exploitation, partly by imparting its ideology to the workers who are led to accept the objectives of capitalism by sharing its utilitarian values. Therefore quite as much as providing objective differences between the several levels of society, capitalism produces an ideology which suggests that hard work, discipline and capital accumulation will allow people in the lower social positions to achieve the higher. The *idea* of mobility is therefore important because it provides the illusion of progress. If mobility in work fails, there is always consumer behaviour as a safety valve. 'The worker therefore feels himself at home only during his leisure, whereas at work he feels homeless.'[15] In Marx's work the real issue involved in social mobility is the dichotomy between the ideology of capitalism which, at its most sophisticated, stresses success and achievement, and the objective situation which allows only for alienation and failure.

The Marxist theory of class adds important demensions to de Tocqueville's. Political change is seen as more than a state of social flux and the emergence of new aspirations and values following the development of democracy: the central feature is the relationship between power and industrial capitalism. If he is less specific about the actual mechanics of political control, Marx's definitions of class and ideology suggest a more coherent approach to what later political scientists have termed the 'inputs' to the political system.

Two major problems remain, however, which need amplification before Marx's theory is seen as one of social mobility. In his theory of class consciousness Marx does not allow much room for analysing how people see themselves in society. Because it is based on their productive relationships, his theory can only hint at how people actually view their social situation. The theory of alienation promises too much and tells us too little. While the concept of 'false' consciousness goes some way towards providing indications of measurements, it is still too crude a category for assessing political behaviour. The second problem in Marx's theory is the absence of any criteria for distinguishing between the economic bases of political action and the institutional context in which politics proceeds, although in his *Critique of Hegel's Philosophy of Right* and in various later works suggestions on the development of bureaucracy on the foundation of increasing division of labour are quite explicit.[16] What is important in Marx's theory is the attempt to trace the character of a particular political system to the class relations in that society. The development of a strong state apparatus is not simply a consequence of the development of capitalism, but of the weaknesses in power of the various social classes and strata. A class which is economically strong (such as the capitalists in nineteenth-century England) will need the state apparatus less, while classes which are economically weak (the peasantry in France or various social classes in Germany between the sixteenth and nineteenth centuries) will require it to represent them. 'They cannot represent themselves, they must be represented. Their representative must at the same time appear as their master, as an authority over them, as an unlimited governmental power.'[17] This important relationship between various class formations and the nature of the political system will be discussed later. Here it is important to note that in spite of these formulations, Marx did not pay particular attention to the actual mechanics of political organization and therefore even if we accept his analysis of the social foundation of political development, it is still necessary to formulate a theory to take account of social relations within institutions and of the precise methods by which politicians and bureaucracies control societies.

Both of these issues are faced by Max Weber, Vilfredo Pareto and Gaetano Mosca. In many respects Weber extends de Tocqueville's analysis of democratic and aristocratic politics and Marx's theory of class. Politics is not based directly on economic interest, though classes are, and neither can be understood without the additional concept of status. A status group is normally a community, if often amorphous, and a status situation consists of 'every typical component of the life fate of men that is determined by a specific, positive or negative, social estimation of honour'.[18] If class rests, as with Marx, on economic interest (but does not relate to social community), status relates to the life styles which define particular groups. The nearest approach to this in Marx was the concept of class consciousness, though this has problems when applied to inter-group relations. Political parties are part of a different dimension again: though they may in part be based on class and in part on status groups, essentially they are located in 'the house of power'.

The importance of these definitions is clear enough for the study of mobility. People may be mobile in three ways—by changes in their occupation, by shifts in status and by alterations in political ranking. Weber therefore provides the basis for distinction between occupational mobility, status mobility and political mobility. A man may improve his occupational ranking by getting a job which requires greater skill, involves more control and carries with it a higher income without necessarily gaining in status vis-à-vis other status groups. On the other hand he may belong to a high status group while his occupational ranking is low (low wages, low control of job routine, low skills). In politics both these dimensions are actively confused. A political ranking may depend equally on low occupational prestige and high community status. The ex-coalminer may become a member of the cabinet precisely because he was a coalminer: in certain circumstances high political status will derive partly from low social status. The question of whether it will depend on the cultural context is a significant issue which is discussed below.

But for political analysis the important question is not simply that of who gets to the top, and how do shifts in social stratification affect the political system, but how power is itself defined and distributed. In other words, for an adequate analysis of the relationships between mobility and political change we must have some conception of the political system itself—its degree of centralization, the existence of a bureaucracy, the whole issue of political legitimacy. Each of these issues is discussed in some detail by Weber. Although it is probably true, as Professor Talmon has suggested, that 'The self-sufficiency of secular society and social mobility are . . . closely interconnected',[19] the development of the complex modern state with its rule of law and bureaucratic rationality has a long history with antecedents which are only marginally connected with social mobility. For Weber there are three basic types of political system—those based on tradition, charisma and legal domination. Historically these are always found in combination, but the tendency in modern society has been towards legal domination. Its main characteristics are (a) an administrative machine conducting official business under legislative control; (b) a legal and administrative order that can be changed by legislation; (c) authority over all persons and most actions taking place under the state; (d) the power to use force within this area if such power is granted by enacted statute. The main characteristics distinguishing traditional from rationally legal societies are the increasing differentiation of the structures and the substitution of statute-based law for traditional appeals to legitimacy. Charismatic authority (the acquisition of power by a man who uses his personal appeal as legitimation) is likely to occur in times of trouble when the presence of a messiah or superman is thought necessary to rescue the state from peril. Although charismatic figures will generally emerge in crisis or transitional periods, certain societies may be prone to semi-permanent systems of domination based on charisma. (In the earlier part of this century many parts of Latin America with a caudillismo tradition of political rule suggest the difficulties of absorbing charisma into rationalistic or legal systems.)

The details of Weber's typologies of political systems cannot be elaborated in a brief text on social mobility,[20] but their importance must be stressed in continuing a comparative tradition commenced by de Tocqueville. With Weber social mobility is not the prime factor in the transformation of political order as it appears to be in Burke, nor are societies simply moving from feudal aristocratic orders to capitalist oligarchic ones as in Marx. The way in which the transition takes place depends as much on the development of legal and economic rationality, the relationship between traditional political organizations and party structures and other pervasive economic and ecological factors. In Weber these factors are picked out separately and dealt with systematically. The importance of a typology as an aid to classification is elaborated by case studies showing development. Although actual statistics of mobility are never given, the conditions under which they may be important and the definitions necessary for analysis are carefully considered. With Weber the systematic study of the relationship between social stratification and political change can be said to have begun.

Out of his analysis there is one further consideration studied at length by Weber that is vital for the study of social mobility. Until now we have discussed the idea of social mobility as a significant factor in the development of modern political systems without specifying how the values associated with mobility came to be established, nor indeed what those values were. In debating with Marx, Weber tried to show that changes in values were not necessarily derived directly from changes in economic activities and productive relationships but that there was at least the possibility of mutual interaction. He was concerned with outlining what values were associated with capitalism and how these values emerged. If at times he seemed to suggest that changes in values actually produced capitalism, elsewhere he indicated that the evidence was less clear. But the central issue was to isolate the values themselves, their origins and their development, and by comparative analysis suggest that some value systems 'had an accelerating and others a retarding effect upon the rationality of economic life'.[21] Much of Weber's work on culture was therefore concerned with religion and economic change and in particular the evolution of particular sets of religious beliefs that led from Calvinist asceticism to the 'spirit of Capitalism': 'For when asceticism was carried out of monastic cells into everyday life and began to dominate worldly morality, it did its part in building the tremendous cosmos of the modern economic order ... Since asceticism sought to remodel the world ... material goods have gained an increasing and finally an inexorable power over the lives of men as at no previous period in history.'[22]

This discussion of religion and economic action, as well as the parallel discussion on the development of legal rationality and bureaucracy, has great importance in the subsequent development of the theory of mobility and the question of the motivation and ideologies of social factors in processes of change. To analyse the political consequences of social mobility we have to know more than the mechanics. The concept of mobility itself with its attendant values of success, the lowering of social barriers and prestige, is a key element in the whole debate. It can even be argued that for some societies and sections of societies the concept or sense of mobility is even more important than being actually mobile. If the Utilitarians provide the ideology of the capitalist-democratic state, Weber suggested how this ideology was related to changing social processes. The idea of success, of entrepreneurial ability and of hard work derived from the emancipation of monastic asceticism, but 'Victorious capitalism since it rests on mechanical foundations, needs its support no longer. The rosy blush of its laughing heir, the Enlightenment, seems also to be irretrievably fading, and the idea of duty to one's calling prowls about in our lives like the ghost of dead religious beliefs.'[23]

But although Weber's distinctions between class, status and party and his analysis of religion and social change added appreciably to the study of social mobility, two further dimensions still required exploration before the full groundwork for modern studies had been laid. The first of these extended Weber's concepts of culture by looking at the ways in which values and status-situations affected each other; the second developed the Marxian concept of the ruling class and Weber's analysis of organizations by suggesting ways in which élites were recruited and how stratification changes affected political organizations. How people come to see each other, the social system and their place in the system is obviously a topic that interested all of the nineteenth-century theorists, but few of them tried to outline a method for studying the actual process. In part, of course, the idea that people measure themselves against others and that this assessment affects their political behaviour, is not new. In his study of the French Revolution de Tocqueville noted that 'it was precisely in those parts of France where there had been most improvement that popular discontent ran highest . . . Patiently endured so long as it seemed beyond redress, a grievance comes to appear intolerable once the possibility of removing it crosses men's minds.'[24] The realization that others were improving their lot while for the majority conditions remained static or improved only marginally acted to inspire revolt.

In Durkheim's writing this theory is expanded. Two of his best-known studies, *The Division of Labour in Society* and *Suicide* have as their basic theme the breakdown in established order effected by the increasing fragmentation of tasks, occupations and values. Because there is no coherent set of values, men are obsessed by individualism which in turn means constant measurement against other men and in terms of material goods. Durkheim's concept of 'anomie' (normlessness) centres on the collapse of recognized codes and communities and the compulsion inherent in industrial society to establish status in terms of a ladder of social ascent. 'What could be more disillusioning than to proceed toward a terminal point that is non-existent, since it recedes in the same measure as one advances?'[25] The problem with industrial society is the total fluidity of aspirations. 'What is needed if social order is to reign is that the mass of men be content with their lot. But what is needed for them to be content, is not that they have more or less but that they be convinced that they have no right to more.'[26]

In *Suicide* Durkheim spelt out the consequences of the capitalist ethic in terms of suicide rates. For the present book, this work is important for its emphasis on 'cultural dominance' in influencing suicide rates. All societies have suicides, but Protestant, industrial and urban societies have more and suicide from a particular motive related to a sense of normlessness. 'The state of crisis and anomie is constant and, so to speak, normal. From top to bottom of the ladder, greed is aroused without knowing where to find ultimate foothold.'[27]

There are two important issues here. The first is the concept of collective culture which, although faintly absurd in the manner framed by Durkheim, is important as a parallel to Weber's stress on the development of national character and on cross-cultural comparisons. The second is the idea that in modern societies individuals are forced to seek new relationships to guide their conduct and that failure to establish these relationships leads to situations of anomie (suicide being the extreme end-product). Although Durkheim himself assiduously avoided any use of social psychology it was through the work of later psychologists and their adaptation by sociologists that the concept of anomie linked to reference-group theory became important in analysing social mobility. If Durkheim recognized that a society based on the values of mobility produced failures, it was left to other sociologists to define failure and the reactions to it. It is worth noting, however, that in most of his writing Durkheim was optimistic, believing that the ideals of mobility and success would take second place to attempts at creating new communities and solidarities. 'The division of labour presumes that the worker, far from being hemmed in by his task, does not lose sight of his collaborators, that he acts upon them and reacts to them.'[28] The normal state was solidarity, the abnormal anomie.

Mobility and political organizations

So far we have discussed the various definitions advanced to account for the existence of social mobility and its wider social consequences. It remains to examine the effects on political organizations themselves. In this again a strong tradition is to be seen moving from Burke and de Tocqueville through Weber and Gaetano Mosca to Michels. De Tocqueville, we have seen, believed that the upheavals in America and France would produce an even greater concentration of power than had been found before. But like Weber he saw this as a process that had begun in the middle ages, reducing feudal diversity and local autonomy and progressively eliminating all those centres of privilege (guilds, estates, families and other associations) which acted as agents of decentralization. The main factor leading to decentralization was the idea of equality, which in turn produced the tyranny of rule by public opinion. 'The foremost or indeed the sole condition required in order to succeed in centralising the supreme power in a democratic community is to love equality, or to get men to believe you love it. Thus the science of despotism, which was once so complex, is simplified and reduced, as it were, to a single principle.'[29] Consequently the state eliminates its competitors by taking over their power and responsibilities and at the same time transforming the institutions of society into democratic organizations.

The result is to stress the importance of internal mobility while giving greater power to the central administration. In armies, for example, the change from aristocratic to democratic selection is bound to increase the pressure of war. Aristocratic officers did not require military adventures to increase their status, but in the democratic army the 'idea of advancement is almost universal' and therefore the ambitious soldiers desire war 'because war makes vacancies and warrants and violation of that law of seniority which is the sole privilege natural to democracy'.[30] De Tocqueville is perhaps the first to note the importance of the military as an agent of social mobility[31]. He further argues that to prevent wars a strict control over the army by the central administration is necessary. This control is made possible by co-operation with senior officers and by ensuring their status in terms of civil honours as well as military.

Bound up with this process is the increasing importance of bureaucracy as a vehicle of control and therefore the pervading importance of committees of specialists and administrators at the top of national institutions. Though de Tocqueville sees this, it is Weber and Michels who spell out the implications in terms of organizational structure. De Tocqueville thought that democratic forms of government would not lead to equality of opportunity within the political system but to the establishment of a new aristocracy with wide powers of control. Weber emphasized the conflict between democracy and bureaucracy inherent in the political institutions of industrial society. In his treatment of bureaucracy he saw the ultimate triumph of legal rationality. If the traditional political figure had been one who had to combine in himself all administrative and 'political' powers (the political equivalent of Samuel Johnson's 'whole man'), under industrial societies management became the responsibility of professional administrators and 'politics' increasingly the prerogative of 'demagogues'. 'Since democracy has been established, the "demogogue" has been the typical leader of the Occident . . . Modern demagoguery also makes use of oratory, even to a tremendous extent, if one considers the election speeches a modern candidate has to deliver. But the use of the printed word is more enduring. The political publicist, and above all the journalist, is nowadays the most important representative of the demagogic species.'[32] Beyond this the nature of political action is changed by the institutions in which it takes place and the kind of people it recruits. Under non-democratic structures the politician did not make his living from politics and thus there was less need for internal political structures guaranteeing promotion and security. But 'for loyal services today party leaders give offices of all sorts— in parties, newspapers, co-operative societies, health insurance, municipalities, as well as the state. *All* party struggles are struggles for the patronage of office, as well as struggles of objective goals'.[33]

There is thus a functional conflict between the need within political parties to provide spoils for the faithful and the apparently irreversible trend within the state to provide administrative specialists and an efficient bureaucracy. In practice, however, the political parties too have developed their cadres of trained management, and demagoguery goes side by side with organization. Given the close link between high state and commercial offices and the party leadership, the political parties, by developing oligarchies, provide an avenue of social mobility. At the same time their committee structures ensure that 'mere demagogues' are eliminated in favour of demagogues with some administrative experience.

In the American party structure the need to provide largesse for loyalty is more embedded in the system than it is in Europe, with patronage at the hands of the president, senators, state governors and the party boss. It is the boss, described by Weber as a 'political capitalist entrepreneur', who is the key figure in the party machine. Because his task is to provide funds he brings attitudes of management efficiency to the recruitment of politicians. 'The boss has no firm political "principles"; he is completely unprincipled in action and asks merely: What will capture votes?'[34] On the one hand— for senatorial and presidential elections—he will engineer the selection of candidates from any social background who seem a good electoral bet; on the other—to help run the party machines— he will create a strong, efficient bureaucracy with career administrators. Although elections are ostensibly democratic, they are engineered by the political bureaucracy operating very much like a huge commercial undertaking. If the American is the extreme case in Weber's examples of modern political organizations, the principle of administrative control of party machines is found in all democratic countries, though more effectively in Germany than in Britain or France.

The details of this thesis were elaborated by Robert Michels in his study of European political parties where the connection between large-scale organization and increasing bureaucracy is more specifically stated. 'Organization implies the tendency to oligarchy

. . . As a result of organization, every party or professional union becomes divided into a minority of directors and a majority of directed . . . With the advance of organization democracy tends to decline.'[35] In principle, political parties are no different from other bureaucracies, though their ideological base may produce particular tensions. If at the top control is in the hands of political bosses, lower down the pressure for status 'corrupts character and engenders moral poverty. In every bureaucracy we may observe place-hunting, a mania for promotion and obsequiousness towards inferiors and servility towards superiors'.[36] Democratic political parties may start off with ideological commitment to egalitarian ideas and may even have impeccably democratic procedures, but once they attain any measure of success and develop large organizations they will be subject to the same oligarchic and bureaucratic tendencies as other organizations. Michels notes 'two regulative principles' in modern political organizations:

> '1 The *ideological* tendency of democracy towards criticism and control;
> 2 The effective counter-tendency of democracy towards the creation of parties ever more complex and ever more differentiated—parties, that is to say, which are increasingly based on the competence of the few.'[37]

Michels' emphasis on oligarchy raises more general questions about the recruitment of political élites. Vilfredo Pareto[38] saw two major strata in a population, the lower stratum and the élite. which he subdivided into a governing and non-governing élite. His main interest was with the governing élite but he argued that it would probably be found that in most societies the richest, most knowledgeable and talented would overlap at the top and that the upper political classes were also the richest: power and wealth went together. However, for the purposes of this study Pareto's main importance is in his attempts to account for changes in élites. These hinge on his conception of psychological aptitudes for rule (which he called 'residues'). Élites change in two ways: individuals rise from lower classes to augment a declining aristocracy, or whole groups are replaced because they have become decadent. Revolutions occur because of increasing decadence at the top and by the development of superior qualities among sections of the lower classes. Unfortunately there is very little specification of how these shifts occur, nor from which lower sections the new élites are likely to be recruited. Thus although Pareto suggests analysis for political mobility (and also for the development of a systematic sociology), his usefulness is limited by the lack of precision in his psychological categories.

In many ways Gaetano Mosca is more relevant for sociological analysis, mainly because he places greater emphasis on environmental and structural factors as influencing the quality and behaviour of the élites. In contrast to Pareto his analysis is more comparative and distinguishes between mobile and immobile societies, modern democracies being far more mobile than any previously known. The circulation of élites is due partly to the existence of opportunities for upward mobility and partly to the creation within a society of alternative power groups who can effectively compete with the ruling class. This in turn posits wider social changes—in religious beliefs and behaviour, economic structures and scientific knowledge—which brings Mosca's analysis much closer to Weber and even Marx than Pareto, though he had a pronounced antipathy to all forms of socialism and materialism.

The studies discussed above raise most of the problems that confront the modern student of political change. In terms of the ideas which galvanized a mobile society, de Tocqueville, Weber, Marx and Durkheim suggested many of the antecedents and cultural consequences. In terms of the definitions of the changing social structure Marx, Weber and Mosca isolated the relationship between economic class, status and political prestige. In terms of the organizational consequences most writers contributed something to the study of political democracy and totalitarianism. But in many respects their analysis stopped short for lack of evidence and it is the spelling out of theory in terms of the evidence that helps to clarify the theory.

It remains to summarize the main outlines of the relationship between social mobility and political change as viewed by the founding fathers of sociology. All writers were agreed that something very dramatic had occurred at the end of the eighteenth century and the beginning of the nineteenth which affected the stability of politics. These changes were seen partly in terms of the increasing fluidity of the system of social stratification and partly in terms of the machinery of government. Commerce, industry and the increasing division of labour had produced new social groups whose relationships to each other were largely dictated by the new values of success and economic achievement which capitalism brought with it. But the new systems of stratification called for new patterns of power. *Which* patterns these would be were dictated partly by the changed economic and social system and partly by the past socio-cultural heritage. But the central feature of the new politics was the emphasis on specialized administrators and the increasing centralization of power. Within this power structure the complexities of a society based on increasing division of labour and the specialization of economic functions calls for its own status hierarchy. In spite of the emphasis on democracy and popular consent the political system becomes increasingly hierarchical and oligarchic. Social mobility provides the value-system of the new society but it is one which is circumscribed by the increasing immobility of the institutions of power.

But from de Tocqueville and Marx, who were viewing the origins of industrial society, to Weber and Michels, who saw it after one hundred years of growth, there are differences in interpretation which owe as much to the ideological tempers of the writers as to the particular historical periods in which they wrote. These differences remain with us though it is important for sociological analysis to attempt an integration of various approaches.

2/Political Systems and Social Stratification

The assumption behind this book is that 'social mobility' is important for the study of modern political change for three reasons. First, the concept of mobility is one that has important cultural implications and thus consequences for the ideologies of political parties, governments and electors. In part this is related to concepts of egalitarianism (which often means equal opportunity for success rather than a levelling-out of living standards), liberalism, the 'open society' and utilitarianism. The Protestant ethic, the 'opportunity state', a 'property-owning democracy' and the 'rags-to-riches' saga, all are part and parcel of the rhetoric of modern societies. In a negative way—by their emphasis on equality and hard work rather than social status and occupational mobility—the Communist states share part of this culture (and of course in terms of their actual changes in stratification show even higher rates of upward mobility). Since the English Civil War and the Protectorate the concept of social mobility and rule by an élite of the economically successful has been a dominating factor in Western political ideas and has recently become important throughout the world. Thus quite apart from the statistical incidents of mobility the idea itself is an important element in the development of political culture.

Secondly, the development of highly differentiated social structures has helped to produce political organizations, in parties and governmental institutions, which have changed the entire pattern of political élite-recruitment and the participation of the mass of populations in political affairs. In part therefore this provides an important area for studying the process of mobility within institutions, but in part it is also an exercise in assessing the ways that politics responds to the factors outlined in the first point above and the third below. Following Max Weber it is important to distinguish within the political framework two major categories: social mobility through political institutions (i.e. access through politics

29

to other socially prestigious positions); and political mobility, or the movement from high to low or low to high levels in the political machine itself. Because both of these imply an assessment of the flexibility or rigidity of the political institutions some consideration of political organizations themselves is also necessary.

Thirdly, the increasing differentiation of social structures accompanying economic and technological development creates stratification changes. Old occupational categories die out, new ones are created, some groups become prosperous, others decline in status. Social mobility is concerned with these shifts in stratification and must deal with several issues: the relative occupational divisions, the pattern of measurement of social status, the cultural relationships of different status and occupational groups and changes in these relationships. Above all, for the purposes of this book, such social changes must be examined from the point of view of political attitudes and behaviour. To what extent are political attitudes related to living standards or community cultures or job situations or wider ethnic, religious or national cultures? And to what extent are central political organizations a consequence of shifts in social stratification?

Running through these broad distinctions is the contention that if political science is to assess effectively interrelationships between ideologies, organizations and systems of stratification it must be able to evolve satisfactory comparative methods of classification and interpretation. In other words, before we can have a 'theory' of human behaviour or institutions we must be able to test some hypotheses in one of the few experimental laboratories the social scientist possesses—that of cross-cultural comparisons. The basic guidelines for a systematic comparative sociology were laid down by de Tocqueville, Weber and Durkheim, though in the twentieth century their approaches have been more than supplemented by developments in political science, anthropology and mathematics. In this chapter and the next we explore the main outlines of a comparative approach to the relationship between political change and social mobility, and in subsequent chapters develop this analysis in the context of industrial and developing countries.

The development of political structures

Weber's contribution to comparative sociology lies partly in his attempt to develop systematically a method for analysing changing social institutions (the law, bureaucracy, cities, economic structures and political parties) and partly in his effort to account for the development of capitalist ideas by examining the increasing secularization of religious values. But it would be erroneous to conclude that for Weber these were separate exercises: the attempt to distinguish between the various components of a social system and the dynamics of social change was part of a total endeavour. The issue was an historical, perhaps even a social-evolutionary one. Why did certain societies develop capitalism and others not? And beyond this the specific questions of the nature of capitalism, democracy and industrial society required precise analytical treatment. In part the conditions for the development of this treatment are found in the writings of Durkheim, in particular his *Division of Labour in Society* and *Suicide*.[1] In the first book Durkheim develops the fairly obvious economic fact that as societies industrialize the distinction in tasks and specialities increases. This analysis has obvious parallels with Weber's discussion of increasing specialization in bureaucracies and the structural machineries attending the growth of capitalism. In *Suicide*, however, Durkheim attempts a more ambitious task; to isolate incidents of suicide according to cultural and structural characteristics. This stresses that comparative analysis requires typologies and classifications as well as a systematic testing of statistical data against chosen variables. Together Weber and Durkheim provide the groundwork for this exercise.[2]

As our study is concerned with the relationship between mobility and politics we cannot here summarize the whole field of comparative political sociology. It is, however, important to outline the general conceptual tools used in the analysis of political systems before we approach social mobility in a political context. Most contemporary political science has divided the study of politics into three categories: culture, function and process. The first deals with the values of societies as institutionalized in social relationships, either (as often used by anthropologists) as indicating the sums of historical and intellectual processes, or (as more generally used by political sociologists) as the values and norms affecting particular sets of relationships. In the first sense the concept is used as being almost synonymous with 'the entire way of life' of a particular society or group of societies, in the sense that we may speak of 'Russian culture' or 'Latin American culture'. In the second usage culture is defined by particular levels of action. We may thus talk about British Catholic culture, meaning the way in which the beliefs and institutions of the Catholic Church affect the lives of its British adherents and also the way in which particular British social relationships and other cultural characteristics affect these beliefs and institutions in Britain. It is obvious that for political analysis both have their importance although in practice the second definition is more useful.[3] In comparative political analysis this second use is often employed in an attempt to isolate the values of traditional and modern societies, and thus has many affinities with Weber's exploration of the Protestant ethic, or Marx's of the 'fetishism of commodities'. It also has close relevance for the investigation of values associated with social mobility.

The second category—function—again has both broad and narrow definitions. In its broader use, function tends to mean the way in which institutions within a particular society do different jobs which, taken together, hold the society together. Thus it may be argued that the function of polygamy in a primitive society is to provide security for women in a world where the men are frequently killed off in battle. Unfortunately one would only have to find another society where there was polygamy but a shortage of women for this explanation to become suspect. As Goldschmidt[4] points out, using this definition of function means that we can only interpret a society's institutions and beliefs in terms of what that society says they stand for. Consequently, he argues that it is more useful to employ an alternative definition of function which sees two major functions performed in all societies: '(a) The work-jobs requisite to the fulfilment of the biologically based needs (and their cultural derivatives) of the population for survival, and (b) The organizational devices necessary for the preservation of collaborative action demanded by these work-jobs.'[5] Developing from this framework it might be possible to distinguish, as Etzioni does, between universal human requirements, particular historical and cultural determinants affecting the development of institutions, and real choices made by social actors about the nature of beliefs and goals.[6] However in sociological analysis the concept of function has been used rather to specify interrelationships than 'needs'. In politics it has been used to attempt to isolate the basic elements of the political system within a general comparative framework of sociological functions. This problem is discussed below. What is generally important in the development of political science is the attempt to add the concept of structure to function: what the political scientist tries to do is isolate the function within political systems and then see how the various structures implement them. This is rather different from anthropological functionalism which tends to see function either as explaining origin (the American use) or as indicating utility in individual societies (Malinowski and the British).

The third category—process—is more easily disposed of. In general it means simply the way in which things are done and is most fruitfully developed by exploring action in the context of culture and structure. If it is often used as an all-embracing catch-word to mean purely descriptive coverage of what happens, it can more precisely be used as the empirical testing of the various theories and application of frameworks. In particular it is concerned with the ways in which particular groups in society give meaning and direction to their relationships. If Marx's *Capital* is concerned with structures, the *German Ideology* with culture, Engels's *Conditions of the English Working Class* is to do with processes.

One further concept is important though its use is subject to variation. The idea of system was developed in its modern socio-logical form by Talcott Parsons[7] and it owes much to the concept of functions. Parsons defines four basic functions in societies; the maintenance of pattern (institutionalized cultural patterns); integration (sub-system of normative control); goal attainment (the polity); and adaptation (the economy). In part this is an abstract device for locating the basic properties of systems, and in part it is used by E. Evans-Pritchard and Parsons to analyse particular societies or to develop comparative analysis based on certain elements of the system. In this second use comparative analysis is not necessarily an elaboration of the Parsonian framework. When, for example, David Easton discusses the political system he is not simply expanding Parsons's framework to cover in more detail one of the sub-systems: in most essential respects the political system is for him the centre of the social system and all 'external' factors are seen in relationships to this particular exercise.

The attempt to locate the functions of systems (whether social or political) and to trace the development of institutions according to their increasing differentiation of roles and structures is essentially an evolutionary exercise. It probably has two major sources: anthropological-evolutionary theory (itself strongly influenced by biology and recently given its clearest statement in the work of Leslie White, and M. Sahlins and E. Service[8]) and sociological theory on organizations and the division of labour. In its convergence in the work of Parsons evolutionary universals have hinged on the 'achievement' orientations within cultures and on the differentiations of structures. The thesis of structural differentiation has been explored by Neil J. Smelser, and applied by S. N. Eisenstadt, G. Almond and Robert M. Marsh and some of the work based on the Yale Data Program and co-ordinated by the International Social Science Council.[9] In all of these works the relationship between social structures and political change is central. Perhaps the most concise general statement of the implications of structural differentiation for the study of political and social change is by Smelser[10] who attempts to isolate the technical, economic and ecological features that accompany development, all of them implying a progress from less to more sophisticated techniques and a shift from rural to urban societies. Smelser finds three structural elements in the development of modern societies: (i) structural differentiation, the establishment of more specialized and autonomous social units (developed in his case study, *Social Change in the Industrial Revolution*[11]); (ii) integration, which changes character as the social order is made obsolete by processes of differentiation (an argument which is more fully developed by Apter and Eisenstadt and discussed below); (iii) social disturbances which reflect uneven advances of differentiation and integration (elaborated by Smelser in his *Theory of Collective Behaviour*). Differentiation is an evolution from a multi-functional role structure (suggested in its ideal type by some primitive aboriginal societies) to several more specialized structures. Smelser attempts to distinguish this process from its cultural aspects, in particular the values and motives accompanying the creation of differentiated roles. In practice, as we shall see, and as Smelser himself goes some way to demonstrating in his *Collective Behaviour* these distinctions are difficult to maintain, though the attempt may initially be useful for conceptual clarity.

In itself the use of a structural-differentiation model does no more than raise a number of questions about the classification of different societies and also creates frameworks for the analysis of social mobility. The more differentiated a society, the more likely are there to be many levels of class and status and therefore the more complex the issue of defining and analysing mobility. But how we decide which are the important levels is not capable of being discussed within the structural-differentiation framework alone because, as Weber and de Tocqueville made clear, it is the cultural framework which gives mobility its particular meaning. If the *rates* of mobility are related to the rate of differentiation of a society and its economic-technological development, the *significance* of mobility is determined by the perceptions of the actors involved and these are of course derived from the peculiar cultural relationships of a society. This point is best demonstrated by a consideration of two writers who have used a differentiation framework to classify political systems.

In his introduction to the collection of essays edited with James Coleman, Gabriel Almond established an early formulation: 'What is peculiar to modern political systems is a relatively high degree of structural differentiation (i.e. the emergence of legislatures, political executives, bureaucracies, courts, electoral systems, parties, interest groups, media for communication) with each structure tending to perform a regulatory role for that function within the political system as a whole.'[12] The main problem is therefore to isolate the functions of a political system, to determine which structures perform these functions, and to assess the extent to which the boundaries between the functions are maintained by the structures.

Almond claims that the main advantage of these distinctions is to allow us to compare political systems according to functions rather than formal structures. We want to know what institutions *do* rather than simply describe what they appear to be. Unfortunately Almond is not clear what the functions are. He classifies them under two headings: input functions (covering such activities and institutions as pressure groups, elections, mass media) and output functions (covering legislation, policy making, judicial processes). Clearly if we were to use these distinctions as the basis for a classification the important variations would be between those societies where structures combine the functions and those where there was strict differentiation. But when Almond comes to make his classifications of modern political systems he is bound to use other, non-functional and non-structural indices. Thus his types of system are:

Anglo-American (presumably based on a linguistic or cultural classification, though it also happens that most of these are more highly-differentiated than the rest); Europe (a geographical category); pre-industrial and part-industrial outside the above (an economic category); and totalitarian (a political-structure category).

The reason for this confusion is instructive. Although Almond sees the importance for a classificatory scheme before embarking on the task of comparison, he also realizes that his classificatory scheme may not help to 'explain' some of the more important differences in political systems. Consequently in his groupings of different types of polity he confuses classification with comparison. If he were to abide strictly by his classification scheme (based on the degree of structural differentiation), he would code all his societies according to the existence of those properties and then compare them in an attempt to assess which had the same properties but differed in other characteristics. Thus if it were found that in most respects two societies had similar rates of differentiation but different political ideologies, then the task of comparative theory would be to explain the difference. This in turn would almost certainly lead to an examination of different historical and cultural factors which the framework took for granted. As it stands, however, Almond's attempt at classification and comparison is more confusing than useful.

Classification and comparison

From the point of view of the relationship between social mobility and politics the distinction between classification and comparison is crucial. In some of the earlier comparative analyses of mobility it was argued that rates of mobility were broadly similar for all industrial societies.[13] Although this has recently been disputed, if the statistical comparison holds it tells us little about the social implications of mobility because it totally ignores the cultural framework. For example, in one society the rates of mobility may be high, but a discontent with the availability of opportunities be particularly marked. This may be because the values of the society lay great emphasis on success. In another society with the same rate of mobility (however computed) discontent with social opportunities may be far less marked because the idea of achievement is partly camouflaged by the survival of an ascriptive and hierarchical social order. The actual rates of mobility are clearly but signposts on the way to a systematic comparison of two different cultural areas. How difficult this is to do in the context of political change is suggested by Eisenstadt. His concept of modernization is closer to Smelser than Almond. 'The characteristic features of the associational structure of modern society are, first, the large number of functionally specific and more solidary or culturally-oriented associations; second, the division of labour between functionally-specific and more solidary or culturally-oriented associations; and third, the weakening of the importance of the kinship and narrow territorial bases of specialized associations on the one hand, and the various "specialized" associations and broad ascriptive-solidary groups on the other.'[14] If a little sweeping, at least this provides a working definition which Eisenstadt uses in relation to political systems. The associational structure is defined in turn against various cultural indices. These include the different historical starting-points, the attitudes of modernizing élites, and the temporal sequence of the process of modernization. Within this framework he locates two processes of modernization. The first is continuous structural differentiation, the impingements of broader groups on the centre and the problems arising out of these processes. The second is the ability of the centres to deal with these problems, 'to develop adequate contractual and precontractual arrangements and symbols'. The variables are grouped and regrouped in an attempt to understand the particular features of modernization in different societies. Ultimately he concludes that the development of an adaptable political centre *prior* to large-scale modernization is the surest route to effective modernization.

Unfortunately, as with Almond, there is still some confusion between classification and comparison. Although Eisenstadt is attempting to formulate a theory of political development his classification of levels of development relates in part to economic-historical categories and in part to political-ideological ones. He postulates two phases of modernization, the first of which is divided into three categories (Western Europe, the United States and the Dominions; Germany and Tsarist Russia; Japan) and the second into three (Latin America; revolutionary, nationalist and communist regimes; colonial societies). For most purposes this classification is useless as it tells us little about the relationship between Eisenstadt's use of differentiation and the broad categories he chooses to impose on the societies. His analysis of Latin America suggests where the theory might develop and why, like Almond, he confuses his classification with the need to explain a particular problem.

As a working premise Eisenstadt accepts Karl Deutsch's definition of social mobilization as 'the process in which major clusters of old social, economic and psychological commitments are eroded and broken and people become available for new patterns of socialization and behaviour'.[15] Mobilization is therefore a more dynamic concept than differentiation: if the latter is the formal reorganization of the institutions and structures into new patterns, the former has more to do with the shifts in attitudes consequent on these changes, though they may anticipate the changes. Mobilization, coupled with structural-differentiation and the need to create adaptable central political institutions, is the key to Eisenstadt's analysis. Latin America is interesting for several reasons. It illustrates a rapid social mobilization mainly through urbanization, the growing politicization of 'broader groups and strata' and exposure to the mass media. It displays a structural duality within societies. Political culture at the centre tends to maintain ascriptive, particularistic values whereas normally it would be the periphery which would have these values and the centre would be committed to achievement and success. And there is a lack of widespread differentiation and thus a consequent difficulty in achieving a broad, parallel development throughout countries.

Though this is extremely general it does, for many societies, accord with most of the research to date. However, this is roughly where Eisenstadt stops. Why this should be so is not seriously debated. Because of the generality it is difficult to know where to go from here: descriptive accounts of Latin American societies would fill in the detail but hardly add to the theory. There is however one negative gain, which is important for this study. In effect Eisenstadt tests the structural-differentiation hypothesis against the experience of Latin American societies and finds it lacking in some important respects. He concludes that 'The implicit assumption that existed in many studies (that the less traditional a society is the more capable it is of sustained growth) has been disproved;' and that 'the types of structural differentiation that have taken place as a result of the processes of modernization were certainly not always of the type predominant in the West during its own initial stages of modernization: that is they did not always take the form of the differentiated collectivities in the economic, political and cultural fields . . .'[16] Societies may develop differentiated structures at lower levels without a firm central administration at the top; or they may develop strong administration on a base of low differentiation. Conflicts arise either because the new modern élites come into conflict with traditional, unmobilized sectors, or because a traditional, ascriptive élite is constantly under pressure from the mobile sectors of the increasingly differentiated structures. Eisenstadt's formulation of the problem is rather more flexible than Smelser's in that he finds historical-cultural factors at least as important as the structural features of changes. The difficulty is that the relationship between structure and culture is left unexplored.

What these attempts at developing cross-national frameworks leave us with are certain basic categories for analysis—system, function, structures, processes, culture—as well as certain terms used to define processes—modernization, mobilization, differentiation. These are important for analysis but they cannot be a substitute for systematic elaboration of comparative theory. Obviously before we can develop theory we have to know what we are theorizing about. It has been one of the arguments of this book so far that most attempts at creating typologies and classifications have been part of a concern with how societies and politics came to be what they are today. But it can also be argued that much theory also attempts to be predictive. As with Marx it tries to abstract from the present and the past those characteristics which can be projected into the future. Since 1945 this emphasis has been important in most social science research, partly because of the influence of UNESCO and other international agencies on the issues that social scientists have taken as their prerogative but partly also because these developments have derived from the very real needs of the poorer countries of the world for plans and projections to assist their economic growth. The structural-differentiation model has a predictive tendency built into it though, as we have seen, not a very accurate one. This is because it attempts to project onto societies which are at certain 'stages' of growth those characteristics which marked other societies which industrialized earlier. Eisenstadt's warning is that this may not be a fruitful procedure. If we can isolate the basic characteristics of all societies, as well as attempting to specify those features which are historically derived, we may be slightly nearer to formulating a framework for comparative analysis. The problem is not that prediction is wrong or useless but that it must be founded on things as they are. To know what these are we must be more sensitive to the variations within societies as well as their apparent similarities.

How should we develop a procedure to account for this? It is clear that there are two basic problems in any comparison of processes. The first relates to common characteristics. We might, for example, argue that in industrial societies people react in very much the same way in similar work situations: given the conditions of work, the rules, duties, etc. the French or British or African worker will behave alike. Or, put at a higher level, given a certain level of technological development, any country is likely to face the same problems of organizational scale (that is size of factories or firms). The assumption here is 'other things being equal'. In certain disciplines, especially economics and psychology, such assumptions are regularly made, and it is often argued in favour of some comparative sociology that similar assumptions can be made in comparing societies. There is obviously much truth in this and therefore the task for a comparative sociology of this kind would be to isolate the classifications and make the comparisons by controlling for other variables. As has been suggested above such a procedure would lead back to cultural and historical variables where comparisons produced exceptions. This immediately raises the other kind of comparison. If it can be argued that it is the culture or history of a given society that produces a given interpretation of process then perhaps the task of the sociologist is to compare cultures; that is, to isolate the variations in how things are done and how the accumulated national, ethnic, religious or political traditions of a given society affect how changes are absorbed. In this case the 'international' characteristics are given and, where deviations from cultural norms are observed, these are used to explain the deviations. Broadly speaking this is a more normal method of interpretation in historical studies while the first method is more usual in other social sciences. Sociology is unique in its attempt to combine the two. In a study of the relationship between social mobility and political change it is imperative that they should be combined.

The importance is best illustrated by example. In Max Weber's study of the origin of modern societies he attempted to account for the rise of capitalism in two ways: by tracing the development of structures and by examining the evolution of economic and legal rationality. His studies of the Far East were particularly concerned with the development of some differentiated structures and legal rationality and the apparent failure to develop capitalism or economic rationality. Further 'explanation' of these discrepancies could therefore proceed according to the two criteria indicated above. He could attempt to specify the degrees of differentiation, integration, etc. and compare societies in terms of these indices, or he could trace the development of certain countries in terms of their internal structures, value-systems and then make comparisons. In the study of the pre-capitalist bureaucracies both procedures have been adopted. Eisenstadt[17] attempted to document all of the major societies according to their geographical scope, structural characteristics, value-systems, etc. The procedure is an essential one prior to effective comparison. It does, however, have serious limitations. If classification is based on purely formal indicators (for example numbers in bureaucracies, size of economic units) we have no means of knowing the functions of these units; the bureaucracy of the Pharaohs or of Louis XIV are put into the same compartment because they appear to be similar in scope. We are therefore not classifying according to functions as suggested by Almond but by structures, and structures make no sense unless we can interpret them in terms of their own society's contours and against similarities and differences, within the same terms of reference, in other societies. Thus if we note from our application of a structural-differentiation model that Manchu China had an economy based on irrigation and management, had a central bureaucracy with recruitment by examination and had a ruling ethic which reflected the bureaucratic rationality of the rulers, we have hardly added to Max Weber's observations. If, on the other hand, we note that certain other societies had some of these features in common with China, the task of comparison and, therefore, theory construction becomes possible. But it only becomes possible if we know the level of comparison. To compare the structures alone is uninteresting and valueless.

The alternative procedure is closer to Weber's own, though it has certain similarities with Marx's view of the 'Asiatic mode of production'. In Weber's discussion (though not in most contemporary administrative and organizational studies) the development of particular types of polity is analysed within the terms of the societies themselves. That is, we study the growth of European capitalism out of the disruption of the Middle Ages, the Renaissance, the Reformation and so on. The ideal types are used to locate problems but the particular ways in which they develop are traced within their own cultural terms. China is studied not simply because it suggests a form of legal rationality, but as an ongoing process.[18]

This procedure is developed in two books which derive their theory and approach as much from Marx as from Weber. In his study of Oriental despotism, Wittfogel sought to 'describe systematically man's hydraulic response to arid, semi-arid and particular humid environments' and also to 'indicate how the major aspects of hydraulic society interlock in a vigorously functioning institutional going concern'.[19] In other words Wittfogel sought to trace how particular economic and ecological conditions gave rise to a particular form of government and how in turn that form of government persisted beyond the boundaries of the hydraulic zones and also influenced political structures after hydraulic society had been superseded by commercial and industrial society. The basic elements of the study are therefore twofold. There is direct relationship between economic pursuits and a system of government and there is the identification of particular characteristics of government, cultural and structural, which can be said to continue independently of their economic base. Thus Wittfogel is able to see in Chinese communism something of an 'Asian restoration' or 'a spectacular manifestation of a retrogressive societal development'.[20] What Wittfogel does, however, is to confuse three different exercises. His study of Chinese society under Han and Manchu dynasties is meticulous and thorough, even if the economic base of the political structure is not completely accepted. Beyond this, however, he considers the 'export' of the system, and in many ways exceeds the bounds of his theory. We are given few grounds for judging why Tsarist Russia or Burma were Oriental despotisms of the Chinese type. If economic conditions are the criteria for judging China, why are they not for these other countries? Thus a theory of cultural dominance is introduced without any substantiating evidence except the circumstantial one that these other societies were despotic and had a bureaucracy. Finally when he returns to the characteristics of contemporary Russia and China, Wittfogel is in real trouble. Marxism-Leninism is clearly a Western European ideology, but developed in a practical form in a country which is one of his marginal zones. It is then introduced to China. The characteristics of communism are contrasted with agrarian despot- ism thus: 'The agrarian despotism of the old society which, at most, was semi-managerial, combine total power with limited social and intellectual control. The industrial despotism of the fully developed and totally managerial apparatus society combines total political power with total social and intellectual control.'[21] What is difficult to see in this analysis is the distinction between a continuing social process within particular countries and the introduction of charac- teristics which transcend national boundaries. The issue is thus to what extent is the particular character of Chinese communism derived from the general problems of establishing industry, a 'modern' bureaucracy, and central control under a communist ideology and to what extent is it derived from the particular cultural and structural heritage of Chinese society?

The answer may be contained partly in another study of the same problem. One of the criticisms we have advanced against Wittfogel's thesis is that although bureaucracy is seen as emerging from the development of a particular economic situation (the hydraulic system of agriculture) the concept of Oriental despotism is then transferred to other societies with other economic systems. That it is possible for Wittfogel to do this partly because of an inadequate account of the precise relationship of the bureaucracy to social relations on the land. He treats bureaucracy as being more related to the technological level of agriculture (e.g. irrigation and the supply of water required organization and therefore managers) and rather less to the ownership of land and the relationships be- tween peasants and landlords.

In another comparative study, Barrington Moore[22] focuses rather more directly on the peasant-landlord relationship. The system of irrigation depended on a series of interlocking levels of ownership of land. 'Local landlord families were constantly pres- surising the government to construct water-control systems, some- thing they could do effectively only if some member had an academic degree and the official contacts that such a degree made possible. This type of wire-pulling appears to be the main economic contribution of the landlord, taking the place of direct supervision in the course of the agricultural cycle. Larger projects on a pro- vincial scale were the work of provincial landlord cliques. Imperial projects were the work of still more powerful cliques with a national vision.'[23] Beyond this, landed families kept themselves in business by sending sons into the bureaucracy. 'Landed wealth came out of the bureaucracy and depended on the bureaucracy for its existence.'[24] Thus although the bureaucracy maintained the system at various levels, it did this by co-operating with the landed gentry. The bureaucracy was the locus of national and provincial power, the main avenue for social mobility through its examination system, but it maintained its power by retaining the system of land-ownership, though in part coming to monopolize the position of land-ownership by itself being responsible for finding new landlords from out its own ranks. For whatever reason, the links between peasants and the upper classes were considerably weaker, in spite of some artificial connections (welfare policies, police and indoctrination) and clan links.

These weaknesses were exploited by the communists when the Imperial system cracked and the Kuomintang failed to make radical agricultural changes. 'The Communist regime forged a new link between the village and the national government. It became evident to every peasant that his daily life depended on national political power.'[25] The destruction of the landed classes and the bureaucracy was a precondition for the creation of a new order. Thus if we are to trace a connection between Imperial China and the establishment of the Communist state, it is important to see the class relations and their sudden change before we analyse institutional features. The peasants revolted in China because the agrarian bureaucracy was unable to adapt quickly enough and because the distance between its control and peasant needs was so great. What Barrington Moore seems to be arguing is that our analysis of which institutions arise in particular societies must be grounded in a theory of social stratification which must indicate the historical processes behind the ways in which different social groups have come to see each other. This is perhaps another way of saying that the changes which take place within societies do so within certain recognized frameworks: it is not that the over-all structures remain the same (though occasionally they do) but that the ideologies and cultural patterns deriving from earlier structural relationships affect the ways in which people come to see the changes.

As with Malinowski's version of anthropological functionalism this does run the risk of trying to explain change purely within a society's own terms, a risk which Barrington Moore does not quite escape. Comparison is simply putting the societies side by side and pointing out similarities and differences. Though Moore does not quite do this, his comparative method hinges largely on his definitions and descriptions of land relationships. What is required is a framework for assessing which characteristics are common to all developing societies and which are peculiar. By listing the peculiarities Moore avoids the similarities, except in the general sense of noting that some societies had argarian revolutions before the development of commercial-industrial complexes, others industrialized from the base of a traditional power-structure, while still others had revolutions based on the peasantry after the traditional structure had begun to crack under the impact of industrial commercial pressures. This conclusion is not too different from Eisenstadt's, though the emphasis shifts from the political systems to the agricultural base of the politics. The gain, however, is precisely in the documenting of the changes in the agricultural structures. The type of 'modern' polity and the subsequent social relationships flow directly from the ways in which the agrarian power system was transformed. It is only this level of interpretation and its subsequent developments in later stages of industrial and organizational change that can form a satisfactory framework for comparative political analysis.

From the perspective of the study of social mobility this ongoing cultural-structural process is equally important. Our interest in how mobile sectors affect the political system is directly related to how social relationships within that system are identified by the different social groups. Thus to identify mobility and to trace its political implications we have to have both a typology of different kinds of mobile situations and a descriptive framework for comparing the process in different societies. It is to this task that we now turn.

3/Mobility and Social and Political Consequences

There are probably two ways in which we can view the relationship between politics and social mobility. The first would try to compare the ways in which government and other political organizations encourage or inhibit mobility. The second is to study the way in which mobility seems to influence political behaviour and policies within a wider context of social consequences. Though both of these approaches are important, it is more useful to begin, as we did with comparative political analysis, with a framework for the entire process.

Mobility can be defined in occupational, geographical or cultural terms. For the purpose of this book the criterion of initial importance is social position, though as the discussion in the first chapter indicated this has a wide range of contextual interpretations. For a discussion of the various implications of mobility it is important to be able to distinguish between rates of 'objective' mobility (that is as measured by indices of occupation, power, wealth, consumption, etc.) and the other variables which give mobility its particular significance. Gino Germani has suggested[1] three levels at which we may analyse. The first is the nature, individual (or group) characteristics, and quantity involved in mobility. The second is the intervening psycho-social variables such as gratification/frustration of individuals, acculturation, identification, personal adjustment. The third is the intervening contextual variables such as the structure of the stratification system, degree and rate of economic growth, and the configuration of mobile and non-mobile sectors. This has many advantages over earlier frameworks in allowing both wide interrelationships and analysis of specific types of mobility. (Many studies of mobility have tended to see it largely in occupational terms.[2]) Germani's framework recognizes that mobility may be from different bases, that it may, for example, be reasonable to discuss racial mobility as much as occupational mobility, the former being a dimension of Weber's status-situation.

46

Before we consider mobility in its political context, it will be valuable to examine in rather more detail the usefulness of Germani's framework for further analysis.

Germani's method calls for a matricated data-collecting procedure so that the various components can be clearly identified. This involves specifying the units under investigation and also the type of relationships to be considered. The basic (or independent) variables considered are those which specify the type of mobility as regards rate, dimension, characteristics and quantification. This type of analysis is characteristic of most studies of social mobility, which isolate one characteristic as a criterion for mobility (for example occupation or income) and then measure the rates and frequencies of mobility.[3] The types of mobility chosen are potentially very great, though in practice certain types may be more significant than others in certain social contexts. For example, it may be relatively uninteresting or insignificant to rank different kinds of religious affiliation in eastern Scotland as indicators of mobility, whereas in many parts of the United States this may be particularly important for developing a real picture of social differences. Whatever indicator is used, however, it is important 'that the social impact of mobility should be *specifically* related to *specific* types of objective mobility'.[4]

It should be noted here that many sociologists have gone some way beyond Weber who distinguished three forms of rank—class, status and power—and have classified ranks by education, religion, race, income, occupation, political affiliation, sex, age and other characteristics.[5] Although all of these can be shown to be in some measure indicators of status, they represent very different kinds of status, with very different levels of hierarchy. Sex, for example, may have four levels: successful men, unsuccessful men, successful women and unsuccessful women, but these levels are likely to have many different meanings (or even orders) depending on different societies and communities. Although this objection holds for all definitions, certain definitions of status only make sense when taken along with complementary levels of status. Logically, however, there is no reason why any dimension which is used as an indicator of status should not be used in analysis. The initial problem is to know why a particular dimension is being used and how it is to be measured.

Mobility may be defined in either individual or social terms.

That is, discussion of mobility may be concerned with the move-ment (which may be variously defined) of individuals; or it may be concerned with impacts on the social structure, or causal changes in the structure, which result from individual and group mobility or which condition this mobility. In the study of politics and social mobility both are important in the analysis of 'objective' mobility, and both will be used in the following analysis.

Although the rates, spread, time-schedule, dimensions and dis-tance of social mobility provide the necessary data from which any analysis must begin the significance of mobility, particularly in its political context, arises because of the other variables which inter-pret its relevance. The first set is used by Germani to refer to cognitive and cultural factors; that is, how people see mobility and the various cultural pressures that affect their perception. There are three main characteristics here. There is the extent to which individuals identify with one group/class or another; there is the extent to which their past cultural/social patterns influence their perception; and there are the ways in which they adjust, in the light of these pressures, to mobile situations.

In many ways this deals with elements of analysis that were discussed in the first chapter. Durkheim's concept of anomie, Marx's of class consciousness, Weber's of status and even Pareto's use of the 'residues' all implied the importance of social reference groups in shaping cognition. Much of Germani's analysis derives from the elaboration of anomie and of reference-group theory which was pioneered by Robert Merton.[6] An individual's experi-ence of gratification or frustration depends on his aspirations, his reference groups and the conflict between his aspirations and their realization. Increased mobility may raise his aspirations and change the reference groups. If these new aspirations are not realized it becomes necessary to discuss frustration in relative terms.[7]

The idea that aspirations may be directly related to concepts of success and be derived from particular cultural values has been further explored by David McClelland who has attempted to ab-stract those specific attributes of success that focus on the sense of achievement.[8] The weakness of this approach is that it related little to interpersonal relations and contributes nothing to the compara-tive study of mobility, except in so far as societies with high levels of achievement-orientation may have high rates of mobility. The more useful exploration of the concept of achievement is raised by

Turner and Lerner[9] who relate achievement values to open and closed systems of stratification and to the influence of mass media. The problem however is very similar to that raised by the debate on capitalism and Puritanism. Which is cause and which is effect? The solution adopted by Germani is to treat shifts in stratification as independent variables and use cultural and personality factors as part of the explanation of variations. Thus we have different stratification changes and constancies and the explanation is in terms of particular contexts and cultural and psychological factors. This is exactly the reverse of McClelland, where the independent variable is the value system and the explanation is in terms of the stratification patterns (though he does not, in fact, actually make this explanation, but rather assumes that the values will create stratification changes).

Finally, Germani posits particular social contexts as intervening interpretations of mobility. These relate to such issues as the rate of modernization of the society, the degree and rate of economic growth, the relationship of mobile to non-mobile sectors, and the structure of the stratification system. This last is perhaps the most important consideration, and relates to the proportion of a population located in each stratum. In the frequently referred to dichotomy of traditional/modern societies, the traditional is seen as having two major strata, most of the population being concentrated in the lower. In modern societies, on the other hand, the system of stratification is seen to be more open, the levels of strata more numerous and the relations between them more diffuse. Most societies, as remarked in the earlier part of this chapter, do not have such clear-cut distinctions, but are combinations of simple and complex systems of stratification. This general profile of societies is important, however, in determining the significance of mobility. For example, the movement into a technological stratum may be much more significant in terms of prestige and status when it occurs in a developing country than in, say, Britain or the United States. In a developing country the technician will be part of a small group with great strategic importance. In an industrial society, although he may have great economic importance, he may have little prestige outside the factory because he is part of a wider group in a less hierarchically structured system. Similarly the rate of economic growth (as opposed to the relative modernity of the society) is important for the significance of mobility. An industrial country going through an economic depression will have fewer opportunities for certain kinds of mobility. Consequently objective rates of mobility may be lower and the resultant frustrations greater. Similarly in a developing country a certain level of modernization of structures and the evolution of attitudes towards achievement may not be matched by economic growth and thus may create widespread frustration among the aspirant sectors. As has often been remarked, one of the major revolutions today is that of rising expectations which are not being met by increased opportunity.

Germani's framework provides a general outline for the consideration of the broad patterns of mobility and the particular consequences for social and political change. Unlike most theories of political change it allows the possibility of keeping certain categories separate for the purposes of analysis while not imposing on processes definitions which actively distort those processes. Unfortunately little of the actual research has been as systematic as this in specifying the variables under consideration. The remainder of this book is concerned with examining various interpretations in the light of evidence from developing countries, communist states and the societies of Western Europe and North America.

4/Mobilization, Mobility and Political Development

Industrial workers and mobilization

For countries in process of rapid change the central indicator of change is perhaps the commitment to, and incidence of, social mobility. Both in the aspirations of the various social groups and in the mechanics of change the society is characterized by shifting social positions, loyalties and political attitudes. But is it possible to identify these processes in order to obtain a clear enough conception of degrees of change? Most sociological theories discussed in the first chapter arose in an attempt to understand the transformation of European feudalism into capitalism. In contemporary developing countries the same theories have been applied and new ones evolved in order to understand what are sometimes very different processes. Their usefulness is best assessed by examining two specific cases of mobility—the emergence of industrial workers and middle classes—in the context of changing political systems.

To characterize industrial workers as socially mobile perhaps requires some explanation. After all, they appear to represent the base-line for mobility: it is from the working class that upward mobility takes place. This assumption, though possibly true for industrial countries, hardly holds for non-industrial ones or for societies in an early stage of industrialization. Mobility, as we have repeatedly stressed, involves cultural factors (attitudes, values, styles of living and so on) as well as purely occupational indicators of role. Any analysis of developing countries must therefore involve mobility as a cultural factor in the process of transition. In political science a distinction is often made in terms of the centre and the periphery, the centre being characterized by the dominating mechanisms of urban politics and the periphery by those areas of society which appear to be uninfluenced or unreached by the politics of the centre. Mobility may as much involve a transition from the periphery to the centre as within the rankings of the centre.

Much discussion of the characteristics of industrial workers in developing countries therefore hinges on definitions of 'centre', 'periphery' and 'transition'. The most perceptive discussion of the issues involved is again found in the work of the Argentinian sociologist Gino Germani and also that of the French sociologist Alain Touraine.[1] Both assume elements of the structural-differentiation framework outlined in the previous chapter though their interests in the ideologies and values of active groups in society provide a more coherent framework within which to discuss the politics of industrial workers in developing countries. It ought to be stressed, however, that their analysis must be seen against the existence of four alternative interpretations of the emergence of industrial workers, elements of each finding their way into the Germani-Touraine framework.

Briefly these elements are: structuralist-social theories of change which aim to trace the development of an industrial working class according to indicators of 'modernization'; mechanistic theories of industrial relations which tend to concentrate on legal and economic issues and the interrelationships between political/legal constraints and the operation of a wage-bargaining system; Marxist-social/ historical analyses of the development of a revolutionary class consciousness (often matched by simpliste rejoinders); and organizational theories of the structure of working-class political organizations deriving from Michels and Ostrogorski. In addition there exist in most countries (though at different levels of sophistication) various studies of economic and political institutions, working conditions, social security and welfare programmes, leisure and educational activities, community development projects and migration which include some element of theory, though normally not related to wider processes, and which amount in the main to useful data that might be used in theories of explication. Finally it should be emphasized that there exist many theories in psychology and phenomenological philosophy which have a direct bearing on the development of ideologies and attitudes and which provide correctives to the more macroscopic perspectives found in most studies of social mobility. These, however, do not appear to have directly influenced Touraine or Germani.

The initial problems in the study of the politics of labour in developing countries are to locate the industrial groups within the wider social structure and from this to assess how this relationship affects their political attitudes. Although Germani's analysis deals primarily with Latin America, his theoretical approach is capable of wider application. The periphery of a society involves those sectors which operate within traditional structures (small communities, occupations isolated from market mechanisms, and the sharing of ascriptive cultural situations). On the other hand the centre, 'the so-called industrial society, is characterized by a high degree of mass participation in the majority of social activities'.[2]

Formally, the transition from traditional to modern society involves three major processes—disposability, mobilization and integration. Disposability occurs when aspects of traditional structures are eroded, displacing individuals and groups from their communities. Changes in methods of livelihood; overpopulation; disruption of communities by famine, war or natural disaster may cause displacement. When these groups or individuals 'respond with added active participation in any sector not foreseen in the preceding structure'[3] one may speak of 'mobilization'. Integration occurs when these groups or individuals are either assimilated into the modern sector by acquiring the features which are necessary for becoming participating groups, or when the structure of society is itself modified so that the mobilized sectors can participate in politics and other aspects of central social life on what are, in effect, their terms.

However, things are never as simple as this. From disposability to integration is an uneven process and most conflicts in developing countries occur precisely 'as a consequence of an incongruence in the aspirations, attitudes, motivations and corresponding behaviour of each group comprising the social structure'.[4] Although many groups achieve a degree of integration by assimilation into the institutions of the centre, many others fail to do so and may either subsist as passive bodies outside centre politics or, under pressure, may direct their activities against the centre or against competing groups. Consequently it is possible to view societies according to rates and completeness of mobilization and integration. These range from those in which mobilization and integration are almost complete (where conflicts are more likely to be institutionalized) to those in which there is extensive mobilization but low integration (where conflicts are likely to become violent). Germani views this classification as a necessary preparatory stage to analysing the origins and processes of particular conflicts that emerge in developing countries.

What has this to do with the politics of industrial workers? This hinges on the distinction between mobilization and mobility. Mobilization is essentially a transitional phase, a movement from one type of society to another. Mobility, as defined by de Tocqueville, Durkheim and others is the characteristic mark of industrial society or, as Germani puts it, 'is precisely the *sine qua non* for integrated participation'. Industrial workers therefore represent the test case of this thesis.

If the thesis is correct we would expect three major divisions in the working class, each with characteristic political values. In the first division would be casually employed workers, recent migrants and poorly paid unskilled workers, each group being characterized by lack of job security and low commitment to the industrial centre. Their values would derive largely from the traditional sectors from which they came or with which, lacking active integration in the modern sector, they necessarily retain strong contacts. In the second division would be those workers whose participation in the modern sector is relatively secure (although their jobs might not be) and whose values therefore are largely derived from industrial society, but whose chances for mobility are blocked. Thus although there is active participation in industrial society, there is little integration and institutionalized conflict is unlikely because of an inadequate power base. Finally, the third division would include those workers whose jobs are secure, whose life-styles are those of urban-industrial society and whose integration is such that conflict takes place according to institutionalized norms. In this last case, mobility, either through occupational and status-levels or by means of income, is considered the norm or at least something capable of achievement within two generations. The precise nature of the relationships between these different sectors does, of course, depend on such basic factors as the rate of economic growth and urbanization, the availability of jobs, the nature of investment and world markets and various cultural factors peculiar to the society. The basic ingredients, however, for an analysis of what Germani calls 'inter-group conflict' are present in the categorization of levels of participation.

If we examine the range of case studies available on the politics of labour in developing countries, the usefulness and limitations of the model are immediately apparent. First it can be argued that three basic components are present in Germani's analysis: structural changes (differentiation moving to reintegration); value orientations moving from ascriptive and particularistic to achievement-based and universalistic; and conflicts between various status and life situations. The way in which industrial labour frames specific political attitudes will depend on the speed, spread and security of creating an industrial and urban sector. According to Germani's typology, therefore, one expects situations in which industrialization proceeds rapidly, creating a large-scale transfer from rural, traditional occupations to industrial and urban ones. Although initial reactions to economic change may be traumatic and even so violent as to include the breaking of machines and destruction of crops, these are speedily replaced by the creation of industrial institutions and mechanisms for routinized conflict. The classic examples are, of course, England and the United States. (In Latin America, Germani sees Uruguay as being the nearest case to full integration.)

The political characteristics of labour movements in the early stages of development of these countries may include random militant protest but this protest is likely to stabilize after the rapid growth of the industrial work force and to transform itself into the formalized conflicts which characterize the contemporary British and American labour scene. In countries which industrialized at a less even pace or which did not experience large-scale demolition of traditional land structures, such as France, Italy or pre-revolutionary Russia, the period of anarchic revolt continued for a longer period, producing more militant labour movements which attacked more radically the political system. In the end when they, too, became subjected to the same institutional pressures they still acted on the basis of a more self-consciously revolutionary programme. In both of these classes, however, it might be expected that those labour organizations which catered for workers with the greatest commitment to industrial security, i.e. those with crafts and high skills, were the most successful in incorporating into the unions the values of the 'centre'. If the unions were militant, it was a militant pressure for sharing what were felt to be the rights and privileges of the centre, such as good wages, job security, control of work training, apprenticeships and entry to work as well as responsibility at work, rather than attacks on the fundamentals of the society. Their advantageous economic situation, based on the scarcity of craft labour, assisted their campaigns. It was left to the less secure workers, those in the public transport or general services, to provide more radical industrial action. In no country was this division more clearly seen than in America where the craft unions early formed their own federation, the American Federation of Labor, and where the industrial and general workers split to form a separate national organization, the Congress of Industrial Organizations.

Thus, if we accept Germani's classifications, some interpretation of the political attitudes of recently created industrial workers' organizations can begin particularly by considering the ways in which the values of the centre are interpreted in relation to the emergence of the challenge of the periphery. The importance of the comparison of Western societies which industrialized a century ago with the 'developing' countries of today is not so much that the European societies prefigured the 'developing' countries but that the political situation of labour in developing countries can be seen, in contrast, as more dramatically different, though some European societies (notably France and Italy) give clearer indications than do the usual models such as Britain and the United States. The central feature of late nineteenth- and early twentieth-century England is that industrialization and urbanization proceeded rapidly with steady economic growth so that ultimately almost all the population conducted its politics in terms of the centre. (The exception is of course Ireland which is never 'integrated' in Germani's sense except in the mass transfer of population to England, America and Scotland.) By 1910 and the last Liberal government the trade unions had developed rapidly and were becoming an integral part of the 'Establishment'. (The 1926 general strike simply serves to confirm the impracticality of 'peripheral' politics.) The United States, in spite of the existence of a substantial traditional sector in the South, rapidly became an industrial society with the workers, even more than in Britain, accepting the norms of the centre and conducting their campaigns within the accepted value-system. Trade unions are not revolutionary but are, in Daniel Bell's phrase the 'capitalism of the Proletariat'.[5]

The counter-examples of France and Italy suggest that for the continued existence of a revolutionary working-class movement further explanations are required. In part it might be argued that persistence of a traditional land sector serves to polarize the politics.

But as America demonstrates this is not a sufficient explanation, nor is it sufficient to add that the land structures must also to some extent dominate the politics of the centre: it is doubtful if they are any more dominant in Italy than is the pressure of powerful southern sectors in the United States.

One further factor, religious belief, is frequently advanced. The extremely authoritarian nature of Catholicism is contrasted with the achievement-orientation and liberalism of Protestant belief. As Bertrand Russell has written, if Protestants rebel they form new sects, but when Catholics rebel they repudiate an entire system of beliefs.[6] In political terms this can produce the argument that the ruling Catholicism of France or Italy is replaced by the radical atheism of syndicalism, anarchism or communism. There is, of course, some evidence for this, though Poland and Ireland suggest caution where Catholicism is equated with nationalism. The importance of the religious argument must not simply be based on the value-orientation of Catholicism and its confessional discipline, but rather on the relationship of this to the continued land structures and the system of government. What Catholicism does in some countries (and does not do in, e.g. Britain or the United States) is to provide a cultural reinforcement of the *status quo*. Its ascriptive elements make it difficult for the idea of social mobility to be respectable. The apparent revolutionary nature of working-class politics may therefore mask two tendencies: a genuine attempt to confront the society at all points and an urge to find a solution to workers' demands for integration into the system. In their recent development the communist-directed trade unions of France and Italy have leaned heavily in the latter direction though speaking in the rhetoric of the former. On the other hand many workers continue to support the ruling culture, attempting, perhaps, to become integrated by conforming to established norms. Their problem comes, of course, when the norms are changed by increasing industrialization and then come into conflict with the Catholic values. What happens then depends partly on the flexibility of the Catholic hierarchy and partly on the demands of their role-situations. One of three things seems possible. The Catholic values may change to accommodate a new normative situation; Catholic values and norms may remain distinct but the worker may choose to act in terms of the norms while still formally accepting the Catholic values; or the old values may be rejected and replaced by others (presumably non-Catholic) which seem to be more in line with the norms. During the industrialization of France and Germany Catholic values did not significantly change and therefore most people had to act in one of the two last ways suggested, although subsequently the development of radical Catholic action in France has provided a third choice.

The major distinction between Anglican legitimation of the *status quo* in Victorian England and the Catholic Church in Italy and France lay not so much in the value-orientations of the church, but in the hegemonic nature of Catholicism. There were, after all, many options in Victorian England both within the Anglican Church itself and in the existence of competing religious organizations. In France and Italy the domination of one church was more complete and therefore rebellion against it in atheistic terms affected a wide cross-section of the 'modern' population: the bourgeoisie were atheistic as well as the industrial workers.

The explanation of American integration seems much more clearly based on demography than either religion or land structures. The creation of a society based primarily on immigration and ultimately on large scale internal migration made it difficult for the landed sectors to dominate the culture of the centre. The values of the new state, even for the oligarchs of the South, were those of achievement and mobility. Taken with the increasing differentiation of roles and structures which attend economic prosperity, the American workers saw success in terms of sharing in the rewards of the system.

The important point is that in considering the political attitudes of industrial workers several factors have to be taken together. The pace of industrialization and urbanization, the existence or absence of flexible political institutions at the centre, the source of industrialization, i.e. whether from internal generation of capital and technical innovation or the import of capital, all of these are obviously basic to any study of industrial workers. In addition there are specific factors such as the occupational status of particular workers, the part played by religious belief, the size and distribution of work places (including such factors as community concentration) and the rural or urban origin of particular workers and their commitment to industrial structures. Any study of the responses of workers to the industrial values—and particularly their attitudes to social mobility—may ultimately consider one set of factors to be crucial but this must be done only by specification of these factors in relation to the others. The importance of this is suggested by a consideration of the Latin American evidence against the European.

One of Germani's central arguments is that mobilization and integration into the modern sector may not be congruent. Workers who are involved in a process of rapid mobilization, but in a society where the pace of economic change does not allow for full integration in occupational and political terms into the modern sector, will be divided into the three broad categories discussed above—marginal workers, unskilled and casually employed workers, and well-established (including skilled) workers. Because they are not fully committed to the values of industrial society, as opposed to the general consumer symbols of mass society,[7] the first two categories of workers will respond in non-institutional manners. Their conception of what industrial society is relates largely to the material goods it offers and the social dislocation it produces. Politically, therefore, they are unlikely to accept conventional politics as having any direct meaning. Their sense of mobility is related primarily to the acquisition of consumer goods either as a form of capital accumulation for *rival* enterprise or simply for material gratification. Their social situation, however, makes it difficult to acquire these goods or indeed to find the wherewithal to provide for basic needs. Thus, strategically their political options are few.

'Political religion' may be a solution: certain aspects of industrial society, notably the end products of mass consumption, become grafted on to a syncretic belief which utilizes both traditional beliefs and elements of a 'religion' introduced along with 'modernization'. The most characteristic elements of such 'religion' are the belief in a future society in which social order is restored, along with the acquisition of the material advantages of modern society. At the same time the presence of a charismatic leader frequently provides the basis for group loyalty which overrides the precise beliefs. Politics is the art of creating a future society on the social foundations of the old, with the material advantages of the present under the guidance of a saviour.[8]

In certain circumstances the marginal sectors may engage in more direct political action. Messiahs may appear whose message is convincingly political and in large measure directed against the political centre, even if without any specific political alternative. In practice, however, such action is unlikely to be long-lived unless it is part of a wider revolutionary situation. In Europe the place of the sans-culottes in the French Revolution,[9] the proletarian street fighting in Ireland in the early twentieth century, or the wider range of radical movements in pre-revolutionary Russia suggest that the marginal groups are mobilized as part of wider discontent and never develop any political coherence on their own.

In Latin America the same characteristics are evident. There is no spontaneous organization or uprising of the marginal urban groups but periodically they have been used as part of a wider campaign. In Mexico there is some evidence that these groups became involved in the fighting after the peasants and war lords had taken up arms, but the low level of economic development at the time made them relatively insignificant. In Argentina, however, Perón actively sought to consolidate his power by appealing over the heads of the established urban and rural classes to the growing mass of the urban lumpen-proletariat while the governments of Vargos, Quadros and Goulart made similar attempts in Brazil.[10] In both situations it is important to stress that governments were not responding to revolutionary demands by the workers but actively trying to create a mass base for their struggle with landed interests, the military and sections of the middle class. In both cases the attempt failed though it produced a level of political consciousness and some institutions which survived the régime's downfall. As Germani said commenting on Argentina, 'for individuals coming from the traditional pattern of prescriptive action, to take part in a strike, elect a trade union leader or discuss with an employer represent a real change', and provide a level of participation (even if of a formal kind) which they are unlikely to give up easily. Argentina, with its very great degree of urbanization, has subsequently provided striking evidence of the importance of the relevance of this analysis to the development of political attitudes. The lumpen-proletariat continues to support Perón but as a messianic figure who may return some day and carry on the good work. The established workers in public utilities and transport are more active in resisting the régime (a general strike in December 1966 provided a critical test of political strength) and Perónism is used more as a mobilizing factor (perónism without Perón) than because of any charismatic appeal. Finally the well-paid and skilled workers, whose sense of commitment to the *status quo* is stronger, are reluctant to criticize the régime and they make periodic efforts to co-operate. It is these workers we must now consider.

In all Latin American countries the skilled workers seem to represent a highly militant group, with membership of revolutionary parties accompanying powerful industrial pressure. Though there is some superficial evidence for this, in that these workers do often appear to be the most militant groups, it is important to note the context of their militancy. Industrial workers constitute a small percentage of the total labour force of any developing country, even of such relatively 'advanced' countries as Argentina. The established workers with both labour commitment and relative security of jobs form an even smaller percentage.[11] In most cases, even if they support such revolutionary-sounding parties as the Communist Party or the FRAP in Chile their basic concern is to maximize their wages and stabilize their own work situations in the way that workers in more industrial countries do. But generally there is an important difference: legal controls of labour conditions are much tougher than in Britain or America and therefore the unions have to organize very much with their eye on the ruling political party or military junta. This means that militancy is organized only within terms that are culturally (though not necessarily politically) acceptable at the centre. In Mexico, for example, the major trade union centre, the *Confederacion de Trabajadores de Mexico*, is officially represented as the labour sector of the ruling *Partido Revolucionario Institucional*, and non-CTM unions also have close connection with the government. Over the past forty years the attitudes of unions have reflected closely the shifts in government policy. Strikes have increased under presidents sympathetic to the unions, largely to bring pressure so that government policies become more radical.[12] On the whole the industrial workers have less of a 'class' consciousness than a 'sector' consciousness, identifying themselves with an urban privileged sector against the 'marginal' population who threaten their position by invading the market for jobs. But the political élite recognizes that a conflict between the 'marginal' population and the established industrial classes would lead to a breakdown of stability. It therefore struggles to maintain harmony.

The marginal sectors—by the very nature of their position—are without organization or leaders. Their typically representative figure is Manuel of Oscar Lewis's *The Children of Sanchez*,[13] the would-be entrepreneur forced to grub around for a living on the market stall of Mexico City and Guadalajara. The contrast between his position and that of the established workers is vast. Only 22 per cent of wage-earners are covered by the insurance schemes of the Institute of Social Security and their wages are double the national minimum wage; some industrial workers even get four times the national minimum. These privileged workers have little conscious-ness of class and organize in industrial pressure groups to improve their economic status in the context of a paternalist neo-capitalist society. In contrast, the marginal workers commonly react by violence, indifference, petty entrepreneurship or retreat to the countryside with which they continue to have close personal ties.

Although Mexico has had a violent revolution and is ruled by a party which claims to 'represent' the revolution, this situation is not unique. Alain Touraine has elaborated on Germani's model in an attempt to account for the basically non-radical nature of the working class in Brazil and Chile. The most important issues raised by Germani related to the possibilities open to workers for co-ordinated action and the framework in which they operate. By pro-viding a typology for social change, using indices of modernization which derive from social and political factors, he has at least made a beginning. In his conceptual framework, Touraine relies heavily on Germani but his analysis is founded on a dialectical method, Hegelian rather than Marxist, stressing the character of social movements and their strategic options.

Touraine utilizes the concepts of defence, opposition and totality to define a social movement, and equates these in various develop-mental stages with theories of mobility, nationalism and class relations. As with Germani he categorizes development according to ideal types, defined by the extent and type of popular partici-pation in the political and economic system. He finds three situa-tions in Latin America: the first where a *popular rebellion* directs its opposition against the 'anti-nation', imperialist forces or colonial domination in response to a situation of acute economic depend-ence; the second, where society is already mobilized by a national bourgeoisie or by the state and where social movements are domi-nated by the importance of individual social mobility and 'collective mobility'. Movements are defined in relation to the new inhabitants of the cities and to some extent against the middle class, but the movements take their definitions of 'general interest' from the developmental process already under way in the cities. National unity becomes the main theme and the movements are what Germani defines as 'national popular'. The third situation is where the society is already dominated by the realities and problems of an industrial economy and faces resistance from 'archaic' sectors or social structures. Political movements appeal to the majority of citizens, not only workers, though this populism has constituted a favourable atmosphere for the progress of trade unionism. Movements are directed against those who impede progress, normally the urban and rural bourgeoisie.

In these three stages Touraine sees a progress from consciousness of one's own class to consciousness of the opposite class and finally to consciousness of class conflicts and alliances. As examples of the three types of situation he instances the Mexican Revolution (popular rebellion), the Kubitschek-Goulart régimes in Brazil (national popular) and the combined Socialists in Chile (popular front). For 'distorted' versions of these situations there are the Bolivian revolutions (popular rebellion on the one side and an institutional system partially resting on the middle class on the other); Perónism (extreme nationalism sacrificing economic development and becoming authoritarian); and Uruguay (the lack of economic potential dooms the popular front to maintaining economic stagnation and social immobility). The industrial working class, though always an important element in the development of new political solutions, is hardly in a position to dictate its own terms. In a situation of popular rebellion what matters is a collective mobility which favours militancy and the existence of activists who devote themselves to a movement or apparatus. However, if one refers back to Germani's distinction between mobilization, participation and integration, because most workers have not yet the elementary machinery for participation, the emphasis is on the machinery. (An amusing slogan for Latin American labour could thus be 'No mobilization without participation'.) But this, in countries which are only partially industrialized, is hardly revolutionary enough. Participation is in the institutions of the urban society: as the Bolivian Revolution showed, even a major revolution effected by industrial workers cannot succeed against the combined offensive of the urban middle class and the rural gentry.

In the second type—the national popular—although there is strong 'participation' in mass movements there is only a mild involvement in their activities: trade unions are closely related to the national popular parties and dominated by the political apparatus. As Touraine says of a country with this situation 'Brazilian trade unionism hesitates between independence from the State, which implies a reformist orientation, and the maintenance of links with the State, which condemns it not to be a live social movement'.[17] Here, too, therefore the revolutionary potential of the working class depends on its alliance with radical nationalist forces among the bourgeoisie (Goulart, Kubitschek, Perón). In the third type of situation—that of popular-front solutions—as social mobility becomes possible and fairly rapid, the unions and labour movements cease to be revolutionary at all and concentrate on 'instrumental' aims.

What Touraine does in this analysis is to combine elements of Germani's theory of social change and group conflict with an attempt to develop a theory of class consciousness. In the course of this he had conducted a series of projects which amplify the theory and develop its usefulness in describing precise situations. Perhaps the most coherent of these is his study of São Paulo because it provides an important case of the degrees of transition and also because of the existence of alternative Marxist theories on Brazil with which to contrast it. After noting a distinction between traditional industrial workers (mainly Italian or Portuguese and including a large proportion of skilled workers) whose trade-union behaviour is not different from European, and the new working class (unskilled and consisting of immigrants from the interior), Touraine bases his analysis on the unskilled immigrants.

Migration has three major causes: involuntary displacement from the countryside, acceptance of new orientations towards the urban areas without commitment to them, and an active sense of mobility involving consciousness of social ascent. In turn this produces three levels of attitudes: a search for individual economic advantages with lack of solidarity in the work place, concrete solidarity with work and family groups, and an 'image of society based less on class conflict than on opposition of social levels, more agrarian than industrial'. Among displaced workers he finds two types of behaviour. The first is 'segmented conscience', which is an attachment to some elements of industrial behaviour but at the same time a general acceptance of paternalism and personalization of social relations in work. The second is 'split conscience', the absence of any integration and consequent instability, use of drugs and stimulants, prostitution, etc. In both these cases the urban process is more significant for the workers' orientation than the industrial situation. Workers either adapt apathetically to work demands or seek economic independence by means unconnected with the mass consumption characteristics of industrial societies. Consequently demagogic movements are a fertile field for activity among these groups. In the category of workers who deliberately accept the orientations of urban society there is a certain consciousness of mobility with relative integration attitudes. Traditional submissiveness continues, but there also exists a 'utopian nonconformism'—hope for improvement in the long run. Industrial society is accepted but more for its consumer values than productive or political. Finally there is complete integration accompanied by strong consciousness of mobility.

Trade unionism in São Paulo consequently involves conflict both between workers as a whole and the bosses and also between various categories of workers. The well-integrated workers constitute a privileged category whose interests are partially those of solidarity with the capitalists, both taking advantage of the domination created by industrial and commercial centres and the 'colonies' of the interior of Brazil. An alliance between this group and bourgeois politicians in the 1930s created a form of trade-union structure which makes the newcomer to the town think of the union as a part of the industrial system. Union fees are deducted as tax from his wage, the union is a distributor of 'services' and the expression of an indirect involuntary participation in power. Consequently although the new workers enter automatically into a union system, few are personally attached to it. The older, established workers are shocked by the arrival of large, new non-militant masses. They either try to radicalize them through Communist-based unions (but the two groups have widely-diverging interests) or they work with the state and try to support an ideology of nationalist and political intervention. Either way the workers have little opportunity to be revolutionary. Success in industrial terms only contributes to regional imbalance, the peasants and agricultural workers having little chance of sharing in the fruits of urban industrial action. And within the urban sector the continuation of family and neighbourhood ties as well as the legalistic structure of industrial relations act as a brake on working-class consciousness and maintain 'traditional' attitudes.

In many respects this analysis does not differ in detail from that offered by Marxist theorists such as Octavio Ianni.[15] The difference is the emphasis on the structural causes and on the ultimate revolutionary potential. Ianni sees the structural features of Brazilian capitalism as being the single most important determinant of workers' behaviour. 'The working class was inserted into a political system designed to avoid or to limit the emergence of fundamental social tensions.' The industrial bourgeoisie is the key to political and industrial relations. Although he recognizes the same differences between sections of the working class, Ianni sees the structure of capitalist development as being more crucial in determining the outcome. 'As long as Brazil is in a semi-developed state, the situation is likely to continue. However, this is "transitional". As the capitalist structure approaches its maximum development, the modification of the substructures slows down, the vertical mobility decreases, the industrial bourgeoisie exhausts its possibilities of controlling other groups, the fundamental mechanism of the system begins to operate. During the last few years the proletariat has begun to find its direction.'

Another view of the revolutionary potential of the urban workers in Brazil is that of Azis Simão and M. Lowy and S. Chucid.[16] Both suggest that newcomers to town tend to be reformist in outlook, while those who are more integrated into urban and economic life tend to be more radical and support the Communist Party. It is clear that although this may have limited truth it produces no evidence of the progressive radicalization of the worker under urban conditions. A fairly high proportion of these workers come from Europe in the first instance so that even if they showed any tendencies towards radical action, this may result more from their European political education and experience than from any social and cultural factors in Brazil. (It also begs the question as to whether the Communist Party is 'radical' in this context.)

Further, as Touraine convincingly argues, the workers' movement has only taken a revolutionary direction when it has had to fight simultaneously against personal power in individual firms and against a capitalist system unable to ensure economic progress. And this, in turn, is determined by governmental social legislation which, in response to crisis, tries to provide a rational structure for industry. To date, therefore, the most important stimulant for trade-union activity—and any 'revolutionary' potential—is the government. For the labour movement 'the conditions commanding its birth also determine its reformist line'. This does not, of course, rule out any revolutionary development (the structural factors suggested by Ianni might begin to operate), but it does cast serious doubt on suggestions that the workers' movement is becoming progressively more revolutionary. But this optimistic (and somewhat naive) judgement is characteristic of many Marxist-orientated writers (unless they have pronounced Chinese sympathies when an analysis closer to Touraine's might be made). It is therefore not too difficult to demolish the theory. Henry Lansberger, in an analysis of trade-union leaders in various Latin American countries, demonstrated that, by and large, they were not revolutionary. In Chile he found that the leaders in Santiago were not very radical, 'supporting the idea that ideological divisions lose their appeal in the course of economic development'.[17] In his book on Peru, Robert Payne[18] comes to similar conclusions, while the substantial output of Touraine and Robert Alexander points in a similar direction.

If we read Touraine correctly, the consciousness of the established workers in Latin American countries is therefore directed towards integration into the politics of the centre (which limits its wider radical content) and by emphasis on the status of the sector as a high social group. This is not so different from the African analysis of Frantz Fanon who argues that the urban workers are 'the most favoured section of the population and represent the most comfortably off fraction of the people',[19] though in Fanon's case the strategic options available to the workers are even fewer because of the even smaller proportion of them in African countries. Governments control the unions for three reasons: they fear *coups* effected by workers, they attempt to restrict the rise of wages in the face of economic and demographic difficulties, and they may genuinely fear the reaction of rural classes to the granting of much better living conditions to urban workers. As Latin American history demonstrates, this condition may not last very long after major industrial development has taken place, and even in Africa the privileged position of workers in South Africa and Zambia suggests that industrial workers will rapidly build unions which establish sector rather than class consciousness once they attain a significant proportion of the total labour force.[20]

The middle class

The significance of the emergence of a middle class has always been prominent in studies of political development. Indeed for many historians and political scientists the crucial thing about social mobility appears to be that it produces the middle class which in turn creates political stability. The importance of the middle class, however, and its political attitudes depend, as does the working class and its attitudes, on the social and historical conditions attending the emergence.

In part this must involve definitions of what constitutes a middle class. Essentially 'middle class' is a concept which only has significant meaning in societies in the stages of early commercial and industrial development. Here it will be used loosely to characterize that group of professional, managerial and intellectual workers who are produced by commercial and industrial institutions and who are distinguished from the upper class, normally a traditional landed gentry or aristocracy, the industrial working class, (likewise called into being by economic change but in all early industrial situations defined by wage-earning and also by manual work), and the lower land classes. The importance of there being a middle class is clearly that this group is 'inserted' into the power structure, having acquired prestige, money and a wide area of control over the actual work situation but not, initially, having political power. But if we examine the middle class, a number of comparative problems immediately become apparent. In some African societies such middle classes as exist gain power after independence, but the definition of middle class here must be even more liberal than that we have adopted. The emergence of nationalist parties frequently causes a kind of collective mobility: it is not simply that the middle classes take power, but that lower-level white-collar workers take power and become a self-conscious bourgeoisie in the act. From the inception of the state these middle classes hold power, the traditional landed élites having had their power reduced by the colonial authorities. Is it logical to call this ruling class 'middle', even though professionally its members may do similar kinds of jobs?

On balance it is, and it demonstrates the importance of locating this type of social group (however we define it) in relation to the nature of economic development, the pace of political change and the wider historical-cultural features. In Africa there is a strong case for arguing in most situations that the upper class is in fact foreign: that is, it consists of foreign companies, banks and governments who are largely responsible for generating and controlling economic development. Indeed in developing countries this is necessarily true unless it can be demonstrated that the political élite derive its power from the people or from the generation of internal economic development. South Africa, Zambia, Katanga and Ivory Coast may just have an upper class: most other countries do not. A middle class is essentially a client class: the African political élites are certainly this.

What we are basically concerned with in this section is the creation of a social stratum, hitherto unknown in the particular societies being studied, which accompanies commercial and industrial development. The task of a comparative and theoretical sociological analysis is to discover the extent to which this stratum shares certain common political and ideological characteristics wherever it appears and the extent to which the particular situation into which it is inserted, or out of which it arises, determine its political attitudes and its impact on political organization. The task is not an easy one and, in spite of the considerable importance attached to the middle class in all contemporary political science, very little actual research had contributed to it.

The main sociological contributions are three: Marx's analysis of the bourgeoisie, Weber's of the cultural elements attending the rise of capitalism and Durkheim's of the division of labour. The first stresses the relationship of the middle class to the new elements of political and economic control; the second the values and beliefs which they bring with them into their new social roles; the third the levels of social interaction that are likely to exist as a result of the creation of new economic and political institutions and the way that these institutions can be defined by these levels of interaction.

Marx's analysis of the new bourgeoisie's relationship to the political process is summed up thus: 'The bourgeoisie keeps more and more doing away with the scattered state of the population, of the means of production, and of property. It has agglomerated population, centralized means of production and has concentrated property in a few hands. The necessary consequences of this was political centralization. Independent, or but loosely connected provinces, with separate interests, with separate laws, governments, and systems of taxation, became lumped together into one nation, with one government, one code of laws, one national class interest, one frontier, one customs tariff.'[21] Thus according to Marx the new middle class not only reorganizes the economy, but also the entire political system and the value-system of the society. It simplifies class antagonisms by splitting society up 'into two great camps, into two great classes directly facing each other—bourgeoisie and proletariat'.[22] Its ideology is that of the free market, seeing competition as 'the only possible way in the eighteenth century to open up a new path of free development for individuals'.[23] The theory of utility follows from this and 'the men of the Manchester School' are (in 1847) the 'official representatives of Modern British Society'.

Weber was more concerned with the cultural aspects of the emergence of capitalism in the West. In his discussion of both the development of types of rationality and of the dimensions of social stratification, he was primarily interested in the levels of cognition attached to particular social relationships. The analysis of religion and capitalism emphasized the value-orientations of nascent capitalists. The comparative studies attempted to isolate those values which were dominant in particular historical situations. In Britain, America and Western Europe it was possible to trace a succession of values from the monastic orders, through the Protestant reformers, the Puritans to the Enlightenment and the capitalist ethos of the nineteenth-century business classes. These values came both from a continuous set of beliefs and also from the particular social situations of the believers. It was one of Weber's main preoccupations to decide which were most significant. This consideration is of profound importance in the study of the emergence of middle classes.

Finally, Durkheim's analysis of the division of labour and the distinction between mechanical and organic solidarity is of further significance in establishing the structural and institutional context in which the middle classes operate.[24] Mechanical solidarity exists where there are shared beliefs and values which produce a common set of values affecting all members. Positions are ascribed and prestige-rankings are formalized. In organic solidarity the diversity of the members of society (both their beliefs and social functions) is characterized by a relatively open system in which individuals achieve their positions and where codes of conduct are based on reconciling conflicting interests. Durkheim took criminal law as an index of mechanical solidarity and civil law of organic solidarity. Both societies, and institutions within societies, may be character-ized according to these types and according to the taxonomies derived from them. Consequently the types of social relationships existing in society could be discussed within those frameworks. Middle classes might appear in either organic or mechanistic systems and the particular nature of their beliefs and values might be derived from these situations.

In most respects Durkheim's typology presents the most useful starting point for analysis in terms of formal classifications of the structures in which middle classes operate while Marx provides an important economic-political development perspective and Weber an elaboration of the systems of values and beliefs. Durkheim is of further importance in the specific analysis of the development of political systems in that the rise of democracy, as de Tocqueville showed, involves a shift from an ascriptive structure to one based on associational relationships and level of achievement. Indeed in many ways mechanistic and organic systems are also in straight succession to Aristotle's categories of aristocracies and democracies, the main differences lying in the emphasis providing the typ-ologies. With Aristotle it is the formal property of the system which provides the basis for categorizing: aristocracies are government by the few and democracies by the many. With Durkheim the level of analysis is the basis of social relationships. This form of organi-zational analysis has profound implications for the study of social movements and political parties. As opposed to psychological studies of class—which emphasize attitudes—Durkheim reduces attitudes to a consequence of structure; and with attitudes go beliefs, 'knowledge' and values, all of which are symbolic repre-sentations of social structures. Thus two of the major influences on sociology, Marx and Durkheim share a common position in rela-tion to ideology: identify structures and we have the ideologies.

If we take the middle class in the context of these frameworks its importance for the analysis of political change becomes clearer. Durkheim saw industrialization as a movement from mechanical to organic solidarity. In 'transitional' society there was a search for symbols of cohesion which could only be met by establishing new contractual rules and morals. But 'transitional' societies cannot effectively do this because they retain symbolic orders from the mechanical system. In other words the values that the middle class brings are those of an organic system but one which still exists in competition with the mechanical one. The problem for analysis is therefore the extent to which the system changes in anticipation of industrial development. If changes are slow in breaking down the mechanical solidarity then conflicts are bound to arise in bringing the two systems together. This is a similar argument to that developed by Barrington Moore and discussed earlier. Thus if we follow Durkheim, the political attitudes of the middle class will follow not so much from it simply being a middle class, as Marx seems to suggest, but from the congruence of social structures. Ignoring the deterministic elements in Durkheim's theory it is possible to take the probable structural combinations to indicate what the middle class's political role is likely to be in particular societies in a 'transitional' stage.

Three, quite distinct, countries will suffice to indicate the advantages of developing an analysis of solidarity in relation to the emergence of a middle class along the lines of Durkheim. If we take Britain first, the problems are immediately apparent. The industrial middle class which emerged at the end of the eighteenth century appeared after two hundred years in which the basic social institutions had been gradually transformed. The English Civil War and its aftermath finally ended a feudal system of power and opened the political institutions to the extent that power was shared between landed classes and new commercial ones. The reorganization of land structures in the seventeenth and eighteenth centuries virtually eliminated the 'peasant' as a social category and thus diminished the importance of a poor agricultural sector in politics. Beyond this the imperial and international commercial ventures of the eighteenth century produced a ruling class which was composed as much of traders and bankers as it was of aristocrats. The democratic nature of politics for this group was important in setting the quality of political institutions. For the rest of society the basic form of solidarity may have been still mechanistic, but for the rulers at least it was slowly becoming organic.

The emergence of an industrial middle class provided a new challenge to this political order which it met initially by retrenchment and hyper-conservatism. Strong class consciousness among the new entrepreneurs was a consequence of this reaction. In terms of the basic patterns of living, however, this ruling class, representing the victorious élite of the Napoleonic wars embarked on demonstrable social splendour which it was able to do partly because the new middle class and the industrialists (some of whom were bankers and aristocrats) had created the base for the new prosperity. When reform came it was in a manner similar to that of the seventeenth century: the system was opened wider but the new entrants displayed a similar religious morality as had the Puritan mercantilists of two centuries before. The moral symbol of this new order was partly derived from the ascriptive nature of the older social order, but, more, it was based on individualistic contractual arrangement between the various sectors of the ruling élite. Political values after the 1832 Reform Act increasingly resembled both High Anglicanism and Utilitarianism. (Interestingly enough also, most of the workers' protests were directed largely towards getting a share of the same open system: Chartism was nothing if not this.) The English middle class, therefore, found itself able to enter an existing organic system (and Parliament has never since the mid-eighteenth century been anything else but a pure form of organic solidarity) and at the same time contribute towards providing the moral and political consensus which influenced the working of the system. The main defect in Durkheim's analysis is therefore not whether organic/mechanical systems provide a useful typology, but the consideration of the conditions under which they develop. His analysis is vitiated in his early frameworks by an undue emphasis on continuous evolutionary processes.

This is seen if we contrast Britain with France. In this case the land structures (perhaps of the type of land economy, as Barrington Moore suggests) were not reformed prior to the emergence of major commercial sectors. Indeed the reverse. The mechanistic system operated in a more extreme form during the eighteenth century due to Louis XIV's reforms of the court. The mercantilist and professional classes therefore grew against this system, the French Revolution witnessing the confrontation of the two systems (more serious than in seventeenth-century England where there were basically two landed classes in opposition). The result, however, was not, as in England, the absorption of one into the other, but the perpetuation of different sectors, each periodically vying for power. At no time from the end of the eighteenth century and through the nineteenth century, except for brief moments in 1789–93, 1848 and 1870, did organic systems look like winning. Industrialization did not begin under an organic ruling system but under various mechanistic ones. It is important to note what happened to the middle class in this. The Revolution of 1789 destroyed part, but by no means all of the traditional landed classes; large estates and peasant holdings continued to co-exist. The middle class (and much more tellingly referred to in France as the bourgeoisie) emerged as the central arbiter of political discord, but bringing to its political duties the ascriptive values of a *nouveaux riches* sector. Having been denied power for so long it spent the nineteenth century attempting to consolidate power. It did so, however, in a way that aped the manners of the aristocracy, mouthed the values of the democracy which brought it to power but operated within a tight mechanistic structure. Oddly enough therefore consensus was only achieved by referring to the values of an organistic system but by operating by tight mechanist rules. This is a variation of which Durkheim probably found it difficult to conceive.

Finally, Brazil. As with France, the middle class emerged here under a mechanistic-ascriptive system, but was never in a position in the early stages to command political strength and effect a revolution. This was probably for two reasons. The Brazilian middle class emerged partly because of immigration, and it grew in the context of a foreign-dominated industrial sector. As immigrants the middle class tended to identify with the existing ruling structure. Charles Wagley has noted that they are 'culturally the most conservative sector of Brazilian society . . . fusing with the old traditional upper class to form a new dominant segment of Brazilian society'.[25] Thus the middle class did not act as a lever for the creation of a form of organic solidarity but inserted themselves into the existing mechanistic one. On the other hand the difficulties of maintaining this relationship arose both from the dramatic centre-periphery dichotomies that it created in Brazilian society and from the instability created by over-domination by foreign capital. In an attempt to minimize the polarities Vargas and later Kubitschek and Quadros tried to create central organizations which involved the peripheral sectors in the form of political participation. Sections of the middle class became increasingly nationalistic in their politics and saw some solution to chronic economic instability in a 'developmental nationalism' and identified with, and largely stimulated, the more radical political and economic policies of Quadros and Goulart. Most sections of this class, however, preferred what they had got to the promise of greater gains later on. They consequently supported the ultra-conservative military coup of 1964. The basic political values of this class were, therefore, dictated by the structural situations into which they were inserted. The mechanistic structures were perpetuated by the parasitic nature of Brazilian capitalism and its dependence on foreign capital. The political alliance of Brazilian capitalism and traditional land structures was not broken by the attempted 'new order' of Vargas and his successors and if 'developmental nationalism' is to succeed, probably it must do so only when economic development under foreign capital has reached even greater proportions.

In each of those situations two features provide important explanations for the nature of middle class politics: the structural base operating *before* industrialization took place and the sources of industrial development. If we insert into this the Durkheimian view of mechanical and organic solidarity, something like a prediction of middle class politics becomes possible. (I have deliberately excluded those cases where the middle class is, as yet, not a significant proportion of a population because of a very low level of commercial and industrial development. These should perhaps serve as laboratory tests for the predictions.) The importance of these factors is well illustrated in one case where the middle class never really emerged as a political force at all. In Tsarist Russia industrialization took place under state supervision. Enterprises were set up using state money and consequently the Tsarist régime overwhelmingly favoured the employers who tended to be aristocratic landowners. While the industrial labour force was made available by forced recruitment, the government controlled middle-class employers and the professions through laws and police inspection. In negotiations between workers and employers the government became the sole arbiter of disputes. Thus although elements of a contractual relationship were established, they operated primarily in a mechanistic system. The middle class therefore could only define itself in relation to a central autocracy, without, however, gaining a clear recognition from it. The increasing physical and social mobility of peasants made the formal structure of a mechanistic system difficult to operate: the autocracy claimed to run a mechanistic system but increasingly had little effective power to do so. The central feature was a bureaucracy. When revolution came it was directed both by workers and the middle class against the central autocracy. But the middle classes had neither the power base nor the ideology to lead a successful coup. The ultimate result of the revolution was to clear the system of its aristocratic trimmings but to leave the bureaucracy even more firmly in control. One form of mechanistic solidarity had been replaced by another. The relationship of the middle class to the state was weaker than ever.

If we contrast these cases in the light of Marx's and Weber's analysis of ideology it is clear that there are certain similarities in the values held by the middle class, but that the political nature of these values is very much affected by the levels of interaction between the middle class, the ruling class and the state. What these levels of interaction are depends partly on pre-industrial structural change, the nature of centre-periphery relationships, and the sources of industrial growth.

In modern developing countries there is also an additional factor, not found in those societies which industrialized in the nineteenth century. This is that the 'values' of entrepreneurship are also partly related to 'borrowed' values of high-consumer behaviour which derive from wealthier societies. 'Middle classes' may emerge therefore which are marked by their conspicuous consumption rather than their entrepreneurial ability, the entrepreneurial functions being performed by governments or foreigners or immigrants. In all these cases, the middle class may be characterized by its preference for a wider mechanistic social structure although its group norms may be akin to Durkheim's organic solidarity. The problem for aspirant middle classes may be that aspirations are not matched by available places. Hence if we return to Germani's distinctions we have mobilization without effective integration. The acquired values of the evolving middle sectors are not matched by their normative situations, which are characterized by mechanistic structures. This process only serves to reinforce the conservatism of those who have 'arrived'. In spite of McClelland's theory of achievement motivation, political attitudes are formed more by structural relationships than the acquisition of values.

5/Mobility and Politics in Industrial Society

Differentiation and political change

With societies in the early stages of commercial and industrial development the relationship between mobility and politics has been seen traditionally in terms of the emergence of entirely new social strata and of the values associated with mobility. One is, therefore, speaking primarily in terms of large aggregates of change. In more industrial societies the fact of mobility is part of the increased differentiation of structures, and the relationship between forms of mobility and politics is often seen much more in the context of political attitudes. It is important, however, that mobility should be examined as a contributory factor in ongoing political processes as well. This chapter tries to do both, and for the purpose three types of mobility are examined as examples of distinct kinds of change. These cases represent the debate on the 'new' working class in Europe; various forms of downward mobility and the relationship of mobility to race, and finally the emergence of new political élites. In the first case the interest is normally on the relationship between technological and consumer factors and the political styles of the working class; in the second the problem is of the incongruity between occupational and status mobility, while in the last the issue ranges from the establishment of a ruling *political* class to political mobility, the movement of individuals up or down political structures. In all cases they represent shifts in political attitudes and have implications for the entire structure of politics.

Traditionally there have been two perspectives for examining the consequences of mobility. As Chapter 2 showed, these include the differentiation-equilibrium studies emphasized by much political-systems analysis. This approach stems from the American sociology of Talcott Parsons and some of his students, notably Neil Smelser and S. N. Eisenstadt. The other approach is the structural-conflict studies deriving from Marx and Durkheim and which recently has dominated the work of many British and French sociologists. The second approach is perhaps most clearly synthesized by the German sociologist, Ralph Dahrendorf.[1]

For the purposes of this analysis the equilibrium theories have two uses: they provide typologies of the levels of interrelationship between political and social structures, and they suggest methods of classifying types of social groups in relation to differentiation. The problems, however, are numerous, and it is difficult to see any study of mobility patterns being able to develop a coherent account of ideology if its basic premise is not to some extent founded on a concept of competing interests. The fundamental sociographic fact of advanced industrial societies is, as the structural-functional theorists emphasize, the increased differentiation of roles and the restructuring of roles. What political theory is concerned with is how these role situations are related to political behaviour and the structure of power. In the early stages of industrialization forms of conflict arise because of the break-up of traditional structures and the creation of new role situations. After a period of time, however, these conflicts may be institutionalized through trade unions, political parties, voluntary associations, pressure groups and the like. The precise pattern of this institutionalized conflict depends, as earlier chapters have stressed, on particular socio-historical factors as well as 'functional' pre-requisites.

As industrialization proceeds, however, the role structures are further diversified and the problem then becomes one of documenting particular role changes and assessing their effects upon the existing forms of institutionalized conflict. Social mobility is a shift in roles, the roles themselves being determined by occupations, status situations (including religion and race) and political participation. One of the characteristic features of advanced industrial societies is that there is not necessarily a direct relationship between these different indices of ranking. The continuing reorganization of industry and commerce creates new occupational roles affecting both the distribution of rewards and the occupational status awarded by community and wider societal indicators. At the same time geographical mobility and urban development create new forms of community and consumer patterns which reflect a complex system of status relationships, not necessarily congruent with those operating in occupational changes. But overriding these, certain status-rankings may persist from earlier social organization which affect relationships and perhaps even gain added importance from particular forms of reorganization (race, for example, would seem to play this function). The real problem, therefore, is to isolate the significant forms of occupational mobility (both in terms of the creation of new occupations and the passage up or down recognized hierarchies) and to assess the relationship of these changes to status situations.

A formal attempt at measuring status and class has been attempted by Lenski and Landekker and elaborated by Galtung.[2] By isolating different dimensions of status they have plotted cases which produce status 'inconsistency'—for example where individuals have high occupational status but low educational or race status, and so on. Although this exercise is important for clarifying concepts and perhaps also indicating where the theoretical issues lie (politically, status inconsistency may suggest political 'deviance' of left or right) it does have two major problems. The first is that most research that has flowed from it is curiously culture-bound. Lenski's categories are largely derived from American situations (where they have some meaning) but outside the United States different elements of status may be significant, and therefore to apply Lenski's categories must involve an element of arbitrariness. The problem is to determine which are culturally determined status indicators.

This immediately raises the second problem which relates to the ways in which we arrive at evaluations of status that may differ from one era of a given society to another. Lenski's model implies a consensus on the ranking of status across an entire society. Unfortunately for sociological research this is not true. Different social milieux may have different status rankings, making it difficult to move from one milieu to another and retain the same status. Any study of status rankings must therefore also be capable of assessing the differences between national dimensions and sectoral dimensions (however we may define a sector). For political analysis, if we accept a correlation between status factors and political behaviour, this is of particular importance in accounting for the degree of support that social movements and pressure groups have in a specific milieu. It is important, in other words, to distinguish between the formal indicators of an entire social system and those which pertain to segments of it. This involves the distinction between the properties of an entire society and the cohesion of sections of a society which may in themselves constitute a system.[3] In fact this requires three levels of analysis: examination of the differentiated role situations such as occupation, status situations, political structure; identification of the symbolic orders of particular milieux; and an assessment of the perception by the actors in these situations of the significance of aspects of the symbolic order for their political identities. In some measure this involves the use of reference-group theory,[4] but it is important to be clear what the differentiated situations are and what are the units of measurement.

We must know, that is, what the changes are *from*, and it is this, perhaps, which most affects the accuracy of measurement and political analysis. Various studies have attempted to account for changes in political attitudes by using indicators of class change. There are two problems: the base-line of change and the comparability of indicators. Runciman for example (see note 4) attempts in his study in 1966 to construct a profile of class structures and political attitudes which uses three factors—class, status and income—as the basic measurement of social differences. But if indicators of stratification represent one set of problems, the use of sources is another. In attempting to compare Britain after 1918 with Britain in 1962, Runciman constructs a profile of class structure and political attitudes in 1918 by using documentary sources such as newspapers and historical accounts. In contrast, his analysis of the 1960s is based on a stratified random sample drawn from electoral registers. As Edmund Leach has observed, there is something curious and unsatisfactory about this methodology. In the first type of profile the methodological issues are basically those of the use of historical sources. In the second it can be argued that a random sample ignores the institutional and communal contexts in which the political attitudes have most impact and from which they draw their meaning. In Leach's words: 'Attitudes are not things which exist in the abstract—they are a response to situations. If you want to know how manual workers feel about white-collar workers, go and stand on a shop-floor and watch and listen: consider the context, the work situation, don't expect sensible co-operation in filling in a form which looks like an application for a United States visa . . .'[5]

But although this is an important general objection to forms of attitude research, its force is offset by the nature of the problems to which it is directed. There is certainly a need both for detailed observation of contexts and for wider surveys: the issue in Leach's criticisms is primarily that we often do not know when we need either. What is important is that the comparisons are made between similar sets of data, and this is often difficult to do because the historical material relies on different kinds of sources and methods of collection. Only when the data has been collected with the meticulous rigour of a Rudé or a Wrigley is it possible to begin to use historical evidence of mass attitudes for comparative purposes. Although deductions can be made with some certainty about structural features, political organization and courses of change, it is rather more difficult to spell out the attitude changes except in so far as these are reflected in institutional forms. Fortunately the institutions and their policies give us very powerful clues. Whatever the institutions have done in the past it does become meaningful to talk about them as representing or not representing attitudes today. In the analysis of political behaviour and institutional change this is all-important. What becomes more difficult to do is to establish the extent of attitude changes and to correlate those with other factors.

The affluent worker and the 'new' working class

One of the most important areas of this kind of change is that relating to the industrial working class. The outlines of the problem are clear enough. Towards the end of the nineteenth and beginning of the twentieth centuries, class structures in industrial societies closely related to forms of political behaviour. Political parties, trade unions and pressure groups became the institutional forms of class activity, even if we accept that the culture of these institutions and their distribution varied between countries. In Britain the Trades Union Congress and the Labour party became the spokesmen of the skilled and unskilled workers. In France and Italy the socialist and Communist parties and the Communist-dominated union federations played the same role. In the United States the American Federation of Labor and later the Congress of Industrial Organizations came to represent labour interests, mainly channelling these politically through the Democratic party. In all countries a sizeable proportion of industrial workers voted for conservative parties. The conflict between crafts' and industrial unions in the United States, though taking a more institutional form, was mirrored in all countries.

As the structure of industry changed, new forms of industrial conflict emerged which brought into being new unions. Often these had distinct political attitudes which took the form of opposition to existing unions as well as other institutions. However in time these differences, too, were formalized. One American writer has gone so far as to see in the unions the true representatives of conservative society, marking a reversal of the trend from status to contract and from mechanistic to organic solidarities. Within society, unions represent the forging of 'a new body of rights and disciplines, which greatly change the substance of a free society. A single bargaining agency collects dues (its own form of taxation) from the worker, without his consent, through the check-off, and has enforceable union security provisions so that the worker must end by being a member of the union.'[6]

Although this exaggerates the extent of union control, for in few countries do as many as 50 per cent of the wage-earners belong to unions, it does put the correct emphasis on the degree to which industrial conflicts produced institutions which not only represented the workers but also controlled them. The mechanics of collective bargaining and labour law produced shadow-boxing between business and workers where contractual negotiations were entered into by large organizations without much response to the democratic pressures of the workers themselves. Even where, as in France and Italy, the unions took a formal militant stance, the pattern of industrial politics was also based on routinized conflicts. National strikes were 'tokens' of protest and usually occurred too frequently to affect the social or political order: the state and the market mechanism operated irrespective of union behaviour. It was therefore not too difficult to demonstrate, as Bell did for America, that labour lost its 'ideological flavour and concentrated instead on market unionism'.[7] Outside America although 'market unionism' was disguised by an ideological covering it was market unionism for all that. Even the growing incidence of unofficial strikes represented *local* responses to *local* market pressures, rather than any major political change. Where attempts were made to create alternative work movements based on the shop floor they were easily destroyed or absorbed into existing organizations.

In formal terms, therefore, whatever the variations in the types of industry, in the range of wages and services or in the varieties of skills, labour politics took a set pattern. Apart from periods of exceptional economic decline the labour vote became predictable. A certain percentage (usually about one-third) voted for conservative parties and the remainder voted for socialist or radical parties. In spite of marginal shifts from election to election this pattern persisted in all major industrial countries, though in some countries (notably Britain and Norway) the percentage of workers voting for Left parties was higher than elsewhere.[8] The basic terms of political conflict tended to include two dimensions—worker-employer conflicts and urban-rural conflicts. In societies with a large proportion of rural workers the total percentage of workers voting Left was marginally lower and the divisions into several political parties greater. Thus political alignments seem to have been affected by institutional factors such as unions and political parties, community factors (rural-urban distributions) and stratification factors.

The study of the 'new' working class has taken place in this context. In some of the earlier studies[9] it was emphasized that increased affluence among the industrial workers was likely to change their voting alignments from left to centre or right parties. If it could be demonstrated that this single factor was the most significant then indeed there would be little room for further analysis. However, the correlation is over-simple. If wealth alone were the single factor in voting, it would be difficult to explain the persistent support for Left parties of some 10 per cent of professional and business groups in Britain and Scandinavia. Clearly if, taken together, institutional, community and stratification factors are important in determining voter alignments, changes in any of these may indicate changes in voting patterns, though probably none of them taken alone is likely to be crucial. Further, the degree of openness in the society at large must also be an important factor in determining how affluence affects voting. In the United States greater openness in the social structure was always a dominant characteristic: 'the American workers were not only given the vote much earlier than their comrades in Europe; but they also found their way into the national system so much more easily because of the greater stress on equality and achievement, because of the many openings to better education, and, last but not least, because the established workers could advance to better positions as new waves of immigrants took over the lower-status jobs'.[10] Within such a system increased affluence must be seen as part of a continuous process of mobility. Affluence may therefore be a symbol of a series of ongoing processes which depend on levels of status, each correlated with particular religious and political alignments. Affluence in a society dedicated to individual achievement is clearly a mark of status; in societies where other societal values are more important it may not be.

In Britain and France the current evidence would seem to suggest that members of the 'new' working class will not necessarily be less radical—they may indeed be even more radical. But this interpretation requires more precise characterizations of the affluent worker. In a comparative analysis of American work situations, Robert Blauner[11] attempted to isolate industrial attitudes in the context of levels of industrial technology and organization. He found four kinds of industrial situations: craft technology; machine-tending technology; assembly-line technology, and continuous-process production (automation-based technology). These technologies are all capable of producing affluent workers and, as Touraine showed in his study of the Renault reorganization at Billancourt,[12] more than one level of technology may coexist in the same factory. The important issue for both Blauner and Touraine is the extent to which technological processes allow workers direct control of the work situation itself. Radical politics may range from militant action on wages and dismissals (as in assembly-line plants) to demands for absolute control over conditions of employment, work schedules, industrial training and even management policies (demonstrated in different ways by workers in craft technology and automation). Thus affluence *per se* is less significant than the degree of skill involved and the extent of work control. In France there is some evidence that the new technological workers favour more militant political and industrial action than the workers in other industrial sectors.[13]

Together these studies suggest the importance of the work situation in accounting for political attitudes. Income and relative affluence do not necessarily lead to non-radical voting. In most studies, militancy seems to be a function either of job security or of absolute job control. But it is also, as Clark Kerr and Abraham Siegel have shown, related to the nature of the industrial environment 'and, particularly, its tendency to direct workers into isolated masses or to integrate them into the general cummunity'.[14] Workers who live in outlying areas are more strike prone than others. Thus even if automation raises living standards and work control, the geographical siting of industry may still have an effect on rates of militancy.

British studies of working-class affluence point in yet another direction. In research conducted in Luton (a town on the outskirts of London with extensive new industrial development), Lockwood, Goldthorpe, Bechoffer and Platt found that voting patterns were imperfectly correlated with affluence. Considering different aspects of affluence such as income, house ownership and consumer behaviour an almost insignificant deviation was found from national class-voting patterns: 'there can be little doubt on these figures that the level of Labour voting was, to say the very least, not lower than that which has been indicated for manual workers generally on the basis of national surveys'.[15] The most important characteristics of Labour voters were their jobs (all were manual wage earners employed in large-scale industrial enterprises), their overwhelming union membership, their life histories of manual work and their working-class parentage. Consumer behaviour, though obviously influenced by their relative prosperity, did not suggest a 'middle class' pattern, but rather increased personal discrimination in the choice of goods. And this, in Britain at least, does not lead to voting Conservative.

In its two aspects, therefore, studies of the affluent worker show two things about their political attitudes. In highly automated plants, as well as in many crafts, workers may, because of their ability to control the entire process of their jobs, have something like middle-class life styles, though their marginal social status may keep them on the political left. On the other hand, affluent workers *per se* are unlikely to change their voting habits because of higher wages: their voting will be determined by work factors, tradition and life styles.

Negroes, downward mobility and political radicalism

One of the important factors of mobility occurs wherever, in Lenski's terms, shifts along one dimension of status are not matched by other parallel shifts. Individuals may move several steps up a particular occupational ladder only to find that they have not gained in social status by so doing. Or, alternatively, individuals may find that although they retain certain aspects of status because of their networks of relationships, their occupational positions do not allow them either the income or the necessary element of work control to permit themselves to live up to their status. Traditionally in sociology this particular phenomenon has been identified with societies in extreme economic growth or under conditions of depression. In societies such as Britain or France in the nineteenth century the appearance of new jobs created large numbers of people who were upwardly mobile in occupational terms even though the status symbols were derived from the traditional ascriptive society. In societies with a dominant rural culture it therefore became necessary for the occupationally mobile to imitate the life-styles of the élite in order to approximate in status. This is essentially a problem of early development.

The predicament of the mobile takes on a different dimension in societies with substantial *racial* minorities. Here—and America is perhaps the clearest case—the mobile Negroes achieve not only similar occupations to the white middle class but also in some respects approximate to their life styles. But for most Negroes it is mobility with an important difference: their success is within Negro communities and if they achieve relatively high status within those communities it is negligible elsewhere. Consequently their sole preoccupation has been acceptance by white Americans, an activity which has been marked by the attempt to acquire the status *symbols* of American society: normally, goods and an indulgence in the 'conspicuous consumption' so vividly described by Franklin Frazier. Thus, for mobile Negroes in many parts of the United States there are three issues affecting status: they operate in commercial sectors which have little impact on the wider American economy; they have little status in relation to other Americans of similar occupational positions, but the pressures to gain status compel them to acquire status symbols and enter what Frazier calls 'a world of social make-believe' in order to gain acceptance. (In this last respect they are not dissimilar to other racial minorities in the United States.) 'The single factor that has dominated the mental outlook of the black bourgeoisie has been its obsession with the struggle for status . . . In escaping into a world of make-believe, middle-class Negroes have rejected both identification with the Negro and his traditional culture. Through delusions of wealth and power they have sought identification with the white America which continues to reject them.'[16]

Even when the activities of the bourgeoisie take on a more fundamentally radical turn, as in certain religious movements—notably the Black Muslims—the norms governing religious behaviour are derived from those that appear to be established in white middle-class society. But it is important to note that the Black Muslims, for all their conformity to white norms, do represent a break into a more conscious Negro movement, the implications of which are incalculable. When Malcolm X was expelled and finally assassinated it was because he sought to extend the 'Nation of Islam' to working-class Negroes. As it stands, 'the nation assists its members to strive for traditional American middle-class values while maintaining their identity with the Negro community'.[17] This, of course, represents a dramatic forward move from Frazier's black bourgeoisie who seek to identify with the white community and have no code of social discipline. As the development of the Black Panthers has shown it is a short step from the Negro consciousness and discipline of the Black Muslim middle class to the mass appeal of 'Black Power'. The problems of occupation and status remain (and most of the black bourgeoisie are still outside the civil rights movement and Black Power). Black Power may provide a focus for some middle-class Negroes (though they tend to be Negroes in white universities and in white-owned industry) but it is probably a middle class which has come up directly from the Negro working class in contrast with Frazier's black bourgeoisie, most of whom 'represent a fusion of the peasant and gentleman'. If this analysis is correct the emergence of more militant politics among the new Negro middle class may be a mark of the emergence of a Negro industrial middle class, which is a comparatively recent phenomenon.

Another major instance of status incongruence is found in areas of declining economic importance or among groups who retain aspirations to high status but see their world crumbling around them. With the rapid reorganization of industry in advanced industrial countries, groups are continually losing occupational status. On its own this is unlikely to have major political consequences. What is important is that these challenges to the occupational *status quo* are matched by major challenges to styles of life and values. Changes in the economy—typically the closure of small business, the uprooting of workers and the growth of large corporations and cartels—are matched by parallel changes in political control, international relations and social attitudes. Economic reorganization brings with it internal migration and the weakening of family relationships; it disrupts communities and sub-cultures and weakens religious loyalties. In this context it becomes possible to talk about collective downward mobility.

Those who stay in the milieu of the old social order or who are forced to live alongside major changes, see their status and life styles challenged and endangered. Their response is typically to uphold a social order which is dying or to support a leader or party appearing to advocate the values they respect even though the consequences of the political programme may be quite different. Political movements based on this type of downward mobility or status deprivation are nearly always right-wing in character. Recently in Europe several movements have emerged which demonstrate this tendency: the NPD in Germany, the Poujadists in France, various neo-Fascist parties in Britain culminating in the support for Enoch Powell in 1968, and status deprivation is a strong element in the appeal of Nationalist parties in Wales and Scotland.

It is in the United States, however, that the most spectacular movement has occurred. Throughout the 1950s, America saw the growth of right-wing movements which clearly demonstrated the relationship between fears for status and political reaction. S. M. Lipset has isolated five issues as contributing to American 'right wing radicalism': status anxiety; the absence of a tradition of tolerance; an 'ideology of Americanism'; 'the lack of an integrated social and political structure'; and the influence of both liberal and conservative climates of opinion.[18] The combined importance of status factors and the ideology of Americanism are crucial to understanding the particular nature of these movements. The ideology of Americanism, Lipset argues, is related to the revolutionary American tradition and to 'the immigrant character of American society, the fact that people may become Americans—they are not simply born to the status'. Thus it is possible to be un-American in a way that it is impossible to be un-British or un-French. Americanism is an ideology which carries with it values of integration. These are the values that the right-wing movements make their own. In the 1968 presidential campaign, George Wallace used the same kind of appeal, though by now the federal government had become un-American along with the traditional figures of intellectuals, Communists and civil rights marchers. Wallace's appeal came, Lipset has argued elsewhere from white workers under threat from Negro immigrants, from some middle-class areas, in rural and small town areas 'which were inhabited by native born Evangelical Protestants', and above all in the South, an area of collective anxiety about its status.[19]

Although the phenomenon of status anxiety and downward mobility may represent the resistance to 'processes of institutional change by virtue of which a more complex and hence more effective division of labour or differentiation has been developing',[20] it is likely to represent a major feature of industrial society for some time to come. The four stages of technological change instanced by Blauner are likely to coexist in advanced industrial societies for many years, and the people suffering under the impact of change may well continue to react by attempting to reconstruct the *status quo ante*. In spite of some sophisticated economic theories of a free market[21] the political ideologies of reaction are likely to be increasingly expressed in terms of the morality, the social relationships and the political order of society rather than its economic policies.

Political and social mobility

Although mobility patterns among either industrial workers or minority groups may reveal pressures on the political system, the recruitment to political office, as well as the structure of power, provide more testing cases of the ramifications of industrial society.

Central to both de Tocqueville's and Weber's analysis of the political structure of modern societies was the contention that democracy was bound to involve the professionalization and centralization of politics. Marxist analysis of politics tended to see the state, bureaucracy and political control largely in terms of dominant class interests, and has therefore been less interested in the actual mechanisms of control. The fusion of a Weberian and Marxist analysis is however nowhere closer than in the work of Leon Trotsky where the conception of a dominating bureaucratic political structure is suggested as one of the major factors in the betrayal of the Russian Revolution. The idea of a political bureaucracy which becomes its own bourgeoisie is never far in Marx's critique of Hegel's theory of law;[22] with Trotsky it becomes central to the analysis of Russian development. Various disciples of Trotsky developed the same argument in relation to capitalist societies (though Trotsky himself was careful not to) and this argument rapidly contributed to a general thesis viewing the development of private industry, the public sector of industry and commerce, as well as government itself, as part of a general tendency towards bureaucratic and managerial control.[23] Clearly this analysis has implications for the study of the locus of power, the selection of élites and the extent to which the system is relatively independent of wider social pressures.

A characteristic of societies with increasing differentiation of structures is that the political system itself has to become more specialized in its functions. This may lead to centralist tendencies, because government becomes the sole co-ordinating agency, but its importance for political mobility is that for both civil servants and politicians specialization rather than aristocratic connections or *general* ability will become major requirements for intermediate grades. At the top, however, particularly among politicians, other factors continue to operate, the most important of which is the party as an agency for recruitment and the selection of leaders. On the one hand the political system demands specialists to supervise particular areas of government business; on the other the more democratic nature of party organizations requires men who will command party and popular esteem. On balance the evidence for most capitalist countries suggests that these requirements are met by professional men and administrators such as bankers, managers, army officers, doctors, school teachers and lawyers, and by career politicians often initially recruited from journalism, trade unions or the party's own bureaucracy. In several countries private businessmen and farmers constitute an important section of politicians, but their significance is reduced by the decline of these sectors, though it is probable that they will continue to constitute an important area of recruitment because of their private wealth. Industrial workers or agricultural labourers have scant representation in parliaments unless there is some formal method of recruiting them, normally through trade-union links with a political party.

The crucial feature for political mobility is the party apparatus. This has formal selection procedures for vetting suitable candidates, which are reinforced by informal arrangements between parties and affiliated organizations. In Britain, Scandinavia, France,

Italy and Germany all socialist parties have trade-union affiliates who sponsor candidates for parliament. Formerly these tended to support trade-union officers or industrial workers for parliament; recently, however, they have increasingly sponsored candidates drawn from the professions. The chances of mobility from lower-paid occupations to high political office may therefore become less for new political generations. The importance of informal prestige groups, such as the Fabian Society in Britain which is overwhelmingly middle class in membership, increases in proportion to the growing professionalization of political recruitment.[24] One of the consequences of this tendency is for political leaders, particularly in socialist parties, to be middle class, and an intellectual middle class at that. This contrasts strongly with the local political parties and the unions themselves whose membership is largely drawn from industrial workers and the lower middle class with a sprinkling of intellectuals.[25]

It is, furthermore, very important to distinguish between local politics and national politics in any study of political mobility. Political systems with a strong element of open competition for office (even if this is a formalized contest) are characterized by an effort to create a local power base which represents a cross-section of local interests. Local and national politics each have a political stratum which consists of groups who are more involved in political action and discussion than the rest of the population, but the local stratum, because of its direct relationship to popular questions, is more widely representative of different social classes and interest groups.[26] Thus, whatever the pressure to produce specialists at a national level, local politics is the nearest thing in modern democracies to open methods of political recruitment. Some of these political figures do move onto the national scene, but this is not their major purpose or function. Within a plural society such as the United States political recruitment will therefore have different levels of selection. At state or national levels the tendency to recruit from business and professional groups, or from the managers of local party machines, dominates over the need to keep recruitment open.

In one sense, however, there are strong similarities of political recruitment at national and local levels. As Dahl makes clear, the pressures on the local political system come from business, education, housing organizations and the like. Recruitment to political office is therefore partly engineered by pressure groups who help maintain local political associations. Because the spread of interests cuts across social class lines, this pressure-group mechanism ensures a wide range of occupations in the political stratum. At the national level the relationship between pressure groups and the financing and organization of the parties is equally great, but the organizations exerting pressures are nation-wide and have much more professional managerial cadres. The tendency, therefore, is for the senior American cabinet posts to be almost exclusively taken by professionals, and by those who are selected because they direct large businesses. Although some of the professionals may have working-class or lower middle-class backgrounds, they gain senior office because of their professional expertise or existing social status rather than because they consciously worked themselves up through the party machines. In Congress, the pattern is more mixed, including a certain amount of recruitment from party managers and local politicians. The important characteristic of American selection is, however, that associations, local parties, pressure groups as well as national and state machines combine to influence the recruitment of leaders. In the United States as well as Britain, for some politicians coming up the hard way political mobility may itself be a stepping stone to social mobility: the backbench politician may be able, because of his political prestige, to gain company directorships, industrial consultancies or the chairmanship of public utilities boards. If this is not achieved, the politician may stay on in politics for as long as possible, Parliament or Congress representing the highest level of promotion he is ever likely to know. The price of social mobility through politics may well be a senile legislature.

The evidence concerning political mobility suggests that as societies develop specialization in economic and social affairs, the political system also specializes. But this does not mean that the power élite necessarily reflects this specialization. What seems more likely is that the bureaucracy will reflect specialization while recruitment to high political office will be based on other factors, notably the structure of political parties and associations, the strength of pressure and interest groups, and provisions within the constitution for selection of cabinet ministers and government dignitaries from outside the party. In systems where the party machine controls all top jobs the chances of upward mobility are much greater than in systems where political leaders have wide discretion in selecting their own colleagues. In the Soviet Union, for example, the Politburo after Stalin's rise to power was overwhelmingly composed of workers and peasants who had made their way to the top through the party machine,[27] a tendency which has been weakened a little in recent years but not to any great extent. By contrast the cabinets of John F. Kennedy and Lyndon B. Johnson were comprised almost entirely of professionals, intellectuals and businessmen, many of whom had previously held no political office. This is not to suggest that the Soviet system does not have pressure groups and that they do not affect the selection of cabinet ministers; the army has an important say and so do constituent bodies of the party such as trade unions and industrial boards. But, with the possible exception of the influence of the army, the real power of selection rests with the party machine, and this is because the party dominates industry, commerce and welfare in a way that neither the government of the United States nor the political parties are able to do. Paradoxically, therefore, where the relationship between the political system and the rest of society is open and based on exchange relationships, recruitment to high office is more likely to make upward political mobility difficult. On the other hand in closed systems where the major instrument of control is the party, political mobility is much more likely, and indeed social mobility itself is greatly dependent on party membership and activity. In both cases, however, increased technological and commercial development leads to greater specialization in the bureaucracy.

It is important to stress here, relevant to the discussion of Russia and Eastern Europe, that the joint operation of party and bureaucracy has not necessarily led to a new ruling class, as suggested by Djilas. Although the increase in numbers of civil servants has been accompanied by growing privileges, there is little evidence that the party has lost power in the process. Indeed the party continues to direct all policy and very little delegation of power is allowed. The Russian objection in 1968 to Czechoslovakian reforms was precisely because this delegation is what the Czechs were proposing. If there is a new class it is that of the *party* bureaucrats who have since the mid-1950s increasingly divested the party of all its democratic features. These bureaucrats are the ruling political élite. What is equally certain, however, is that the rapid economic development of Russia under Communist control has created large numbers of upwardly mobile groups whose positions depend on the unity and stability of the Communist government. In time this feature of Russian stratification has probably taken precedence over other social divisions, in contrast to the satellites of Eastern Europe where ethnic, religious and class divisions are maintained in spite of Communist control and where colonial status makes the munificence of the party appear less generous. There is no doubt that the growing professional quality of state bureaucrats and industrial managers produces tensions between the party bureaucracy and the specialists but to date this new mobile group has not been able to affect any lasting change in the policies and composition of the party élite. When it does it will of necessity affect the legitimation of power.

The strategic importance of political mobility is in direct relationship to the way in which parties or governments are able to ensure control by promising rewards and high office to their followers. In exchange-power systems such as the United States, power is exerted by national élites on the basis of reciprocal arrangements. At the lower levels the political stratum may be recruited from a wide range of occupational and status categories, but the rewards for service are not in the hope of political mobility but in the allocation of local-level honours. Because a plural system has many contestant groups, neither the socially mobile nor political aspirants are necessarily strategic rivals. Rivals come primarily from the party machines and national pressure groups, just as locally they come from the party caucuses and local interest and pressure groups. Political mobility is therefore possible only through the support of one of these agencies. In centralist party systems, on the other hand, political mobility is encouraged through the machine, thus legitimizing aspirations and at the same time controlling them. Socially mobile groups are important only in so far as they challenge this system. In general the processes of differentiation affect most Communist systems as much as capitalist ones and therefore the existence of major clusters of challenging groups is unlikely. With two exceptions. Both the bureaucrats, who have to manage the system, and the military, who have a vested interest in the maintenance of certain forms of order and scientific and technical development, represent challenges to the party. Except in cases of economic disaster, they are likely to be the agencies of political change. The Russian invasion of Czechoslovakia seems to represent the response of the combined strengths of the party and the military against the demands of the bureaucracy. On the other hand, as in the capitalist societies, the bureaucracy may fail to provide an alternative system of government because, like the middle class in Tsarist Russia, its source of power derives from the political centre and its lack of corporate identity makes alternative political action difficult.

6/Differentiation and Political Power

Much of the analysis of mobility and political change has taken place piecemeal. The general observations of de Tocqueville, Weber or Marx have led to particular research without necessarily improving the general theories. As that recent debate in Britain on the 'new' working class indicates, we may be able to produce sophisticated research on one dimension of mobility which does not necessarily add much to our knowledge of political change. This is mainly because it is difficult to know how generalized these conclusions can be. In this particular case two issues seem significant: whether the 'new' workers change their voting patterns, and, if they do, whether this has major consequences for the direction of political policy and the balance of political power. It is important to have evidence on voting changes in Britain, but it would be equally important to know how widespread this change is. And even if the changes (or lack of them) are universal in voting behaviour for similar kinds of worker, we still do not know under what situations they are important enough to affect the political system nor how the influence is likely to be felt. On the other hand, in the study of political *development*, the analysis of social mobility has tended to concentrate on general theories—Germani and Touraine have been taken as more pertinent examples—without offering very much in the way of a systematic framework for comparative research. It is into these two extremes—particularly in industrial countries and generally in developing countries—that de Tocqueville's successors have placed themselves. But if politics is to gain from the study of social mobility it is necessary to provide something of a basis for comparative analysis. It is to this task that we now turn.

Classification of social structures

The classificatory issues in social structure can be derived from the study of structural differentiation. This has three major divisions: the economic-technological features which attend the creation of occupations and industrial and commercial organizations; the differences of status which affect interpersonal relations; and the institutional aspects which influence the manner in which differentiated roles are integrated into total or partial structures. In each of these cases the ways in which changes take place are partly influenced by historical/residual cultural features, partly by functional prerequisites of situations and partly by specific contingency factors. As Smelser indicated in his study of the industrial revolution in England, increased differentiation only becomes important when it seriously disrupts the life styles of large sections of the population.

The initial problem is to isolate the economic, technological, demographic and cultural features which causes this disruption. For societies in early stages of industrialization three processes are simultaneously affecting social stratification: the emergence of new upwardly mobile social groups, the horizontal movement of manual workers from rural to urban and industrial occupations, and the downward mobility or displacement of old élites. In some cases the first two shifts may be due to immigration. In most respects the particular structural problems of an industrializing or 'developing' country can be initially plotted by the use of a typology which isolates these changes in stratification according to whether they proceed together or whether any one change is far in advance of the others. In Britain the displacement of old élites and the emergence of a new middle class took place together, making it difficult for historians to identify exactly which had precedence. In some crucial respects the traditional élites themselves became entrepreneurs. Although the population shifts were dramatic, they, too, tended to accompany changes in the élite and the rapid development of industry. From an economic point of view, the failure to match industrialization with population movements could be disastrous (though it could be solved by more rapid mechanization, as partially happens in Canada and Australia), but to date this has not been an issue: there are always enough people. In many of the developing countries today the problem is of the reverse order. Populations move but new élites do not emerge rapidly enough and old élites refuse to die or adapt. In the United States the old élites also refused to adapt, but it was possible—though at the cost of a Civil War—to concentrate industrial development in one part of the country while the other part retained its traditional structure, at the same time providing much of the migrant manpower for industrial growth. As Barrington Moore has indicated, all of this may be due to the kinds of land structure predating commercial and industrial development, and certainly the complexion of political structures accompanying industrialization would suggest there is strong evidence for such an argument. However, the development of more differentiated structures can be considered in two ways: one may look at the elements of cohesiveness, solidarity and integration accompanying differentiation, or look at those forms of social stratification preceding, and following from, differentiation. The two perspectives do, of course, interrelate, but as much research has emphasized one perspective or the other, it is important briefly to examine their different merits.

The emphasis on consensus and solidarity, characteristic of Durkheim's sociology, is important in beginning the study of differentiation. The major difficulties in Durkheim's thesis relate partly to his biologistic conception of social change and to his simplified view of what society is. Mechanistic solidarity as defined by Durkheim does not represent *all* pre-industrial societies nor are the changes bound to lead to organic solidarity. What *does* happen is that the use of new production techniques, the vast changes in communication and the widening boundaries of social contact progressively weaken community, family and other forms of traditional solidarity. This in turn is bound to alter the basis of consensus and solidarity. In traditional societies of whatever nature patterns of norms and values are closely interrelated. This may imply a mechanistic system such as Durkheim describes (though it does not necessarily) but it is certainly based on less differentiated structures. As the productive technology and communications become more complex so the norms governing particular areas of behaviour become more varied. People's actions in specific situations cease to imply normative consensus because the situations themselves have become so diverse that a societal consensus on all these normative situations becomes virtually impossible. Consensus, such as exists, is found in general national value-symbols and in the norms governing *political* behaviour.

The importance of Durkheim's conception of organic systems is that the idea of contract between different elements of society does replace status, but in most societies probably not for the whole system. It may, for example, affect economic relations but not educational ones. Or it may be found in national government but not local government. But such a discussion only makes sense if Durkheim's concept of 'solidarity' is used for specific situations where large collectivities act together for particular purposes, such as in times of disaster, war or major industrial unrest. In industrial societies it is clearly exceptional because of the divisive consequences of differentiation for total structures, culture and norms. It may be possible to discuss *mechanical* solidarity with some meaning but it is difficult to see organic systems having solidarity in this sense of cohesiveness. Organic systems are held together by contract, consensus, routinized conflict (which is a variant of consensus and contract) or by brute force, but rarely by solidarity, though it is possible that solidarity in the face of danger or threat may produce consensus. This, however, is hardly what Durkheim meant.

The importance of the power structure is therefore fundamental for explaining how societies, which are otherwise characterized by diffuseness, instrumental relations and differentiation of normative situations, are held together. For Durkheim, in a mechanistic system power accrues to those who hold the top of the status pyramid and they do this either by conquest or inheritance. In organic systems on the other hand the power structure is produced by the 'needs' of the different levels of interaction in the system. The state reflects the moral consensus of the social system. 'Transitional' societies suffer because they have not yet found organic solidarity therefore they tend to operate two types of social system simultaneously. The failure of politics is a measure of the failure of moral consensus. At all levels this analysis is unsatisfactory because it does not provide sufficient ground for analysing the effects of power on the social system. For Durkheim, power can only appear as a consequence of particular levels of interaction in society and he does not allow for interaction between the political system and elements of the social system. Consequently he does not help to define power as such.[1]

There are, however, alternative ways of viewing the relationship between consensus and political power. Of course it is true that cohesion and consensus may in some way 'represent' the moral basis of a society and be the sum of the levels of interaction. But how does the power structure reflect this consensus and represent non-political interaction? One way of finding out may be to identify the values of consensus and attempt to establish whether they, (a) reflect the values of particular elements in society and, (b) are derived from historical or structural features inherent in the political system itself. Whether or not we can isolate values in a meaningful way, the problem of identifying elements in society returns us to the units used to analyse interaction. A simple functional model, as Durkheim and most of the structural-functional theorists imply, is based on functional autonomy: each unit in society is of equal importance. But as Gouldner has pointed out,[2] in systems of interaction some elements have greater power than others: A and B may mutually interact but whereas B is dependent on A, A may not have the same dependence on B. Thus in any system of interaction we have dominant and weaker parts. The analysis of political power makes it clear that some elements in society have greater influence over political processes than others and thus the first exercise in isolating political power is to establish which these are. This is very close to Marxist analysis: the state is the handmaiden of the bourgeoisie. But of course logically this is insufficient. By the same series of arguments it is possible to show that the political system can have greater power than the elements with which it interacts. Trotsky was the first Marxist to see the force of this,[3] and this seems to be the logic of Weber's position also: as systems of bureaucratic rationality develop they may come to dominate all forms of political interaction.

The problem for comparative sociological analysis must therefore be first to classify political systems according to degrees of dominance from sub-sections of society and also according to degrees of control by the system itself. Beyond this the important questions are why one form persists rather than another, and whether there is any connection between forms of interaction and the kinds of ideology, values and symbols which dominate at different levels of the system. This is a more satisfactory way of proceeding than classifying societies according to pattern variables and types of value orientation (which Parsons tends to do) or by general social structures which are based on some form of moral solidarity or consensus (which Durkheim does). One of the important issues in the relationship of politics to social structures is to explain values and changes in values and also norms and normative changes. It is difficult to know how this can be done if the initial classifications used assume (because they classify by them) particular combinations of values.

Under this form of analysis consensus may seem to emerge from one sector of society which happens to dominate the whole, or from political formulas which may draw heavily on tradition, or select elements of tradition, for purposes of legitimation but which reflect not the interests of one 'non-political' sector but the interpretation by the political élite itself of the values it considers necessary for maintaining order and power. This latter situation may arise in part from exchange mechanisms between different units but in part also from the logic of the political structure's own development. If we accept that this is possible, and the empirical evidence suggests that it is, then it may be easier to avoid the dichotomies presented by the functionalist, interactionist and the conflict variations of political analysis. In Ideal-type situations it may be possible to find systems which approximate to a perfectly equilibriated society where the interaction of different elements produces consensus without either political domination or terror. Alternatively, in many situations the *opposition* of competing sectors may at best be institutionalized but it is not possible to talk about consensus and system-integration: in Gramsci's terms the opposing forces establish a hegemony of values and cultural styles.[4]

But of course no society is an ideal type and the elaboration of a simple typology which accommodates centrifugal and centripetal tendencies in relation to levels of political interaction allows both for societies in which consensus and integration exist and for those where dual or multiple conflicts permit no consensus. Although this approach implies a system, in the sense of there being inter-related parts, it is not a variation of Easton's model for the political system. In Easton's model[5] the nature of the inputs to the system is of lesser importance than the system's own structure; in our case the inputs are crucial in determining what that structure might be, though in some advanced societies the dynamics of the political structure may override the inputs. This *is* another way of stating the centre-periphery thesis though one which allows that the values of the centre may be derived directly from sectoral interests (the landed classes or the middle classes, or in societies such as South Africa, racial élites); from an exchange between sectoral interests and those accruing from legitimation-mechanisms of the politicians (contemporary Britain is a fair example); and those which seem to derive primarily from domination by a particular type of régime which creates its own client sectors to give it a social power base (the Soviet Union demonstrates this most clearly). Between each of these there are transitional states where emerging sectors attempt to change the foundations of existing power, as in England during the seventeenth and nineteenth centuries; or where political élites may attempt to change their power base by appealing to sectors formally on the periphery, e.g. Argentina and Brazil in the 1940s and 1950s; or where an old form of sector-political control collapses under new forms of sectoral contest to allow the emergence of a new power structure as in China during the mid-twentieth century.

Theoretically it is possible that each of these six varieties of political system may exist in any type of society. In fact increased differentiation and specialization within sectors makes the task of changing the basis of power more difficult, therefore to a large extent making exchange mechanisms between political control and sector control more likely. But it is possible that pre-industrial transformations will, as in the Soviet Union, make political control dominant even after increased differentiation.

If we accept this as a working framework for the study of the relationship between political power and social sectors or classes, the study of mobility and political change begins to take a more coherent form. Firstly, mobility is important politically only if it involves the movement (upwards, downwards or horizontally) of groups which are significant enough to affect the relationship between the political system or elements of it and their power base. This means, secondly, that in many cases mobility may be frequent and involve many sectors without *perceptibly* altering either political behaviour or the distribution of power. Conversely in societies where the power base is very narrow, as in many developing countries, the creation of relatively small groups through upward mobility may have important implications for political stability. Thirdly, in some cases, such as in the Soviet Union or some Eastern European countries, absolute domination over economic, cultural and other social structures by a political bureaucracy may produce sectors totally dependent on the bureaucracy for mobility. The emergence of new professional groups, whose expertise comes into conflict with the bureaucrats, may lead to changes in the nature of the political system—as was demonstrated in Czecho-slovakia in 1967–68 or Hungary between 1955 and 1968—though as the Russian example to date demonstrates this is not an inevitable development. But if such a system does not respond sympathetically to pressures from this new mobile élite, it is likely to be overthrown, as in Hungary in 1956, or resort to even more authoritarian control as in Russia in 1968. What happens must depend in part on the importance of the new élite for the direction of economic and political development and in part on the instruments of control that the ruling bureaucracy is able to command. As the recent examples of Greece and Brazil show, a regime may willingly destroy its own modernizing sectors.

The élite and new sectors

In social systems where power depends either on exchange relationships between the political structure and several élite groups or where political power is largely at the disposal of one, or at most two, élite groups, the emergence of new sectors is clearly of great importance. It is necessary to examine this latter category in order to amplify the typology.

In societies where the political system seems to represent directly the interests of a dominant class or sector, it is important to specify the class bases, whether feudal, racial or mercantile, from which this power arises and the likely threats to the control of the élite. In this context it is worth examining in further detail two recent attempts at providing typologies: those by Stinchcombe and Touraine.

Stinchombe's essay[6] tries to define rural class relations according to types of agricultural enterprise. As most societies which have politics dominated by single-class élites are likely to be agricultural this is the proper place to begin. In Stinchcombe's typology, where pre-commercial societies and community-enterprise agriculture (such as Israeli kibbutz or Soviet collective farms) are ignored, there are five major categories of land ownership: the manorial or hacienda system, the family-size tenancy, family small-holdings, plantation agriculture and capital-extensive agriculture with wage labour (the ranch). The manorial system is the clearest structural parallel to Durkheim's mechanical solidarity: diffusely related tenants hold their land from a manor lord for whom they are obliged to work or provide crops, their legal status defined by their inherent inferiority to the lord. The lord's domain usually produces crops for the commercial market and thus controls the technical culture, while peasant land is used for subsistence. Politically the upper class is dominant, operating in the towns and leaving the operation of agricultural estates to managers. The peasant is 'politically apathetic, backward, and disenfranchised'. He also has little chance of upward mobility in this system; the challenges are likely to come from mobile sectors in the town or from the reorganization of agriculture under market pressures. The characteristic of manorial or hacienda systems (if these last two conditions do not operate) is political stability.

In contrast the family-size tenancy tends to lead to political upheaval. Property rights rest with rentier capitalists but the basic unit of agriculture is the family tenancy. 'The rent from the enterprise is divided according to some rental scheme, either in money or in kind.' Because these forms of tenancy agreements are normally found where the value of land is high, labour cheap, crops labour-intensive and produced in a year or less, the amount of rent produced varies from year to year and thus leads to continual bartering between tenant and rentier. The rentier lives in town, dominates the politics of the centre and has little contact with the lower classes except to collect rent. In the rural areas, on the other hand, the farmers develop high political consciousness under the leadership of richer peasants who suffer the same market and rent problems as poor peasants. Above all, because the rentier class does not initiate technical development and has no control over the technical culture, it is only too apparent to the peasants that they could manage as well without the rentiers. As Stinchcombe suggests, this type of agricultural structure is inherently the least stable of all and has been the foundation of most revolutions. The uncertain status of the more prosperous peasant and the continuous and deep-rooted grievances of the poor peasants combine to provide political tension. In most cases the overthrow of the old order results in the introduction of family small-holdings, though in Communist states attempts are made to introduce collective farms.

The relationships between the rentiers and political power appears to be similar to that existing in manorial systems, in both cases an élite deriving its wealth from the land dominates all political offices and determines what the political values should be. In fact the differences are more marked than this similarity. Under a manorial system social relations are based on status ranks and political power is mainly concerned with sorting out differences between manorial chiefs. There are no other competing élites. Under a family-style tenant system rentier politics has constantly to contend with the emergence of peasant opposition so that ultimately the lords and rich peasants have to come to terms (as in south-east England during the thirteenth century) or the old order is swept away by the force of peasant opposition after large-scale wars. In the first case there is no political mobility within the agricultural system; in the second the rich peasants aspire to replace the rentier lords. (In some areas of South America or South-East Asia the two forms of agriculture coexist in the same country. Political élites are thus drawn from manorial lords and rentier capitalists and it is probably true in most cases that the power of manorial lords is used to buttress vulnerable rentier groups leading to forms of internal policing of restive peasants. But as Colombia, Mexico and Bolivia have demonstrated in different ways, this is a difficult task: peasant unrest in family-tenancies may create revolution or Mafia-style banditry which increasingly destroys the basis of control in adjoining haciendas.)

Of the three remaining categories of land system described by Stinchcombe, family small-holdings need not concern us here. In general these emerge in societies with advanced stages of industrialization or their creation helps to prepare the way for industrialization. In any case they then properly come into the category of political exchange systems and their influence is relative to the power of urban élites. The plantation system, on the other hand, has a master-servant structure and an economic base which often allows it to dominate in poor countries and thus control the political system. Its characteristics are closer to the manorial system than the family tenancy with the important differences that the labour force is based on intensive wage or slave labour and that the crops require several years for growth and consequently a certain amount of capital investment is required. As under the manorial system, the technical culture is controlled by the élite, and the legal differences between the élite and the work force are absolute. In many cases the legal differences are reinforced by ethnic differences: unskilled labour is drawn from underprivileged areas, often the native peoples of a colony or migrant workers from areas where there is little urban work, while the élite is itself expatriate but from a different ethnic group. Occasionally, as in the Ivory Coast, an indigenous élite may be absorbed into an expatriate one, but this is rare. Status, educational and technical privileges are also often reinforced by ethnic divisions. Politically this élite has greater capacity for control than the rentiers of the family-tenancy system, probably because it has control over the technical culture. Government is dominated by landlords and because in most cases the plantations form the basis for a monoculture, there is little competition from aspirant élites. The classical examples are in the Caribbean and Central America, the antebellum American South, Malaya, Java and Hawaii. Where political movements occur among the labourers they tend to be instigated by revolutionary governments or by outsiders, as in Tanganyika in the early 1960s and in Jamaica in the 1940s.

Little needs to be said about the ranch. Although widespread in the American West, Canada and Australia as well as parts of Argentina, Brazil and Mexico, its political impact is less across entire states, though in Argentina the ranch élite acts as reinforcement for other rural élites. Because of the free-floating nature of ranch populations, there is little political action. Historically the attitudes adopted by ranch élites have been determined by their market situations and their relationships to other élites.

This typology, as provided by Stinchcombe, is clearly inadequate in covering all forms of land structure or in providing a sufficient basis for assessing why particular crops are raised under different systems in different parts of the world. But this is less our concern here. What is important in this exercise is that agricultural structures are seen as developing from different forms of land tenure and that challenges to ruling élites can be specified according to both the structuring of agricultural activity and the status-dimensions of the system. The likelihood of mobility and its bases can be seen in this context, and also the possible consequence for élites.

This is, of course, not enough for the analysis of mobility and development. Not only do many challenges to élites come from outside the agricultural structures (indeed they are more likely to) but the typology does not suggest what may happen if the economic base changes in the towns as well as in the countryside. The most important considerations for an analysis of the entire process of mobility and development must rest with the relationships between structural differentiation and economic development, though, as

Stinchcombe's essay and the Marxist tradition indicate, the important issue for the relationship between mobility and political change is the way that differentiation, forms of economic change and historical-cultural features generate perceptions of social structure among the groups affected by differentiation.

Touraine's attempt to do this for Latin America has already been discussed in Chapter 3. The importance of this essay[7] is that it sees political change in terms of the opposition of different sectors; its limitations are that there is no clear conception of social structure. Touraine sees different forms of political conflict emerging at different levels of economic development. Under conditions of economic backwardness and colonial dependence, popular rebellion is instigated by the 'exploited classes' against colonial agents. At a later stage of development 'society is already mobilized by the national bourgeoisie or by the state and social movements are dominated by the importance of individual social mobility or occasionally collective mobility': the conflict between urban sectors and rural sectors is marked, but national unity is attempted under national popular movements. Finally, where society has largely become industrial, popular fronts emerge which define the adversary as those who represent archaic structures such as landed classes and types of bourgeoisie.

There are two major problems here. Essentially Touraine's typology is concerned with the situations in which revolutions of popular rebellions are likely to occur. Although he may be right in this respect, this hardly provides a typology of developmental stages. The structures are seen entirely from the perspective of conflicting groups, not *as* structures. It is therefore very difficult to derive from this classification the different forms of structure that exist at different times in different parts of Latin America. Secondly, and because of this, it is difficult to see how countries which have had revolutions in the earlier stages will look later on: Mexico's revolution is a clear case of stage one but today in terms of economic and political development she is between stages two and three. On the other hand there is no way of deriving from Touraine's typology any explanations as to why revolutions do *not* occur in the different stages for many countries.

Having said this, it is important to specify the kind of framework that we need in order to study the *sources* of mobility, the political attitudes generated, and the kinds of political change effected. For this it is important to have the following: profiles of agricultural structures as well as their sources (e.g. by colonial imposition or slow historical growth—Touraine is noticeably weak on this); forms of urban-industrial-commercial development and their typical internal structures; sources of this development (i.e. whether generated from internal capital accumulation or by foreign capitalists and governments); changes in agricultural structure (whether by land reform, revolution or increased commercial development); the lag between industrial-commercial development and population movements and aspirations; and the composition of political élites, the ramifications of government control and the centralization or diffusion of political power.

Mobility and political change

With such information at our command it should then be possible to identify the central issues in the relationships between mobility and political change. In his observations of nineteenth-century American democracy de Tocqueville argued that the most important difference between an open society such as America and an 'aristocractic' one such as France under the *ancien régime* was that in America the consciousness of mobility was a dominant theme in political culture, but that these aspirations were bound to lead to a centralized form of government legitimizing its power by promising as much to the majority as it could get away with. From our discussion of Durkheim and Marx it is possible to put this rather differently. For any society the political importance of mobility can be seen as having three elements: the structuring of different roles, the symbolic orders governing the interpretations of these roles, and the part played by the distribution of power in affecting the integration of roles and symbolic orders into the mechanism of political control.

In the United States the varieties of role situation are very great indeed and one of the dominant elements in the symbolic order is the stress on role mobility. On the other hand the structuring of roles may unevenly affect the distinctions between racial, occupational, consumer, educational or political roles. Thus although the symbolic orders as represented by values and some normative situations may stress mobility, the structuring of roles may make this very difficult to do in practice. Until recently, as the example of the black bourgeoisie shows, the solution for groups who were mobile through one set of roles but not others was to seize on life styles which were derived from national symbols of values and imitate them. In other societies this alternative may be less clear cut: the mobile along one dimension may not interpret their lack of congruent status as 'deprivation' and their life styles may represent values derived from ascribed order (as appears to be true in Britain) or alternative 'hegemonic' cultures (as appears to be true in Italy).

The way in which these incongruities in role structuring are perceived (and the argument is that the perception is normally derived from the symbolic orders) will affect the impact of mobility on political institutions. Until the early 1960s it was possible for politicians in the United States to assume that mobile Negroes would respond to deprivation of status by channelling their frustrations into imitations of life styles rather than political dissent. They therefore presented no threat to the *status quo*. Since the Kennedy era it is not possible to make this assumption, for Black Power has demonstrated that Negroes are increasingly likely to view their role situations as a matter of group identity and not according to *individual* identification with corporate symbols which have little relevance to their normative situations. In part this is probably because politicians since the Little Rock crisis of 1957 have repeatedly asserted that the national values of mobility and equal opportunity applied to them too. Thus their normative situations, which demonstrate that they do not share equality in all respects, come into conflict with the expressed values of the system. A solution which Black Power offers is the mobilization of the Negro population to demonstrate that as far as status goes they are all in the same situation: the inferior role which their race makes them play according to the day-to-day normative situations reduces their chances of mobility in other spheres. For perhaps the first time the Negro identifies himself not with the roles which white men play but with a common Negro normative situation.

In a very different context the same analytical problems presented themselves in Nigeria between independence and the outbreak of the civil war. The creation of a new state out of three regions with distinct social and cultural structures could only succeed if the symbols of legitimation were universally accepted. In the absence of a common enemy or the accumulated solidarity of a liberation struggle, legitimation could initially only flow from the social positions of the élite and the mass of the population's acceptance of power relationships. With different social structures operating in different regions of Nigeria, but with political élites acting in coalition, the voters' attitudes to the régime were clearly affected by different concepts of legitimation: the mechanistic, feudal solidarity of the north in harness with the mobility-aspirations of the east. It seems likely that this pattern could have survived only if there were certain *common* legitimizing symbols: most societies have strong sections of dissent based on radically different social structures, but they hold together because of agreement on the symbols of power.

In Nigeria the collapse of the consensus, slender as it was, occurred largely because of the loss of faith by the new mobile groups in both the system of advancement and the incumbents of high office. Two events contributed to this collapse: the prosecution for corruption of the opposition political leaders of the Western Region, when it was clear that they were no more corrupt than some of the government ministers, and the successful 'exposure' of government corruption and inefficiency which accompanied the general strike of 1964. When the coup was effected in 1966 its aims were stated to be to 'stamp out corruption and dishonesty in our public life with ruthless efficiency and restore integrity and self-respect'.[8] Unfortunately for Nigeria the results of the coup, which had no noticeably new symbols of political legitimation and order, was mainly to provide a group of army officers with personal mobility routes. The challenge to their legitimacy came twelve months later, bringing with it a challenge to all forms of social mobility, and in particular by relating mobility-opportunities to ethnic monopolies. The campaign against the Ibos, as Hitler's against the Jews, was a mark of the frustration of the immobile in a society where the acceptance of mobility routes had broken down. The Ibo's solution, like that of the Jews, was to retreat to their own territory in which a different pattern of stratification might be developed.

In conclusion, therefore, the implication of social mobility for political change is not that mobility necessarily brings with it a challenge to the political system but that that challenge comes from a recognition by the mobile that their identification in a society rests on interpretations of their role situations which are distinctly different from those which are held by the political élites. This is why de Tocqueville was impressed with American society in contrast to the French. The French Revolution had shown that new mobile sectors were prepared to contest the social order and replace it with one which, though in many essential features not unlike its predecessor, had the merit of having them at the top of it. What had changed most fundamentally was that the legitimizing symbols of society were now split between a bourgeois version of a mechanistic order and the recognition by the same order that other aspirant classes might have the right to challenge the order too. Subsequent French development has shown this to be so from the Paris Commune to the student-worker demonstrations of 1968.

In the United States on the other hand, with the notable exception of the old Confederacy states, the system recognized individual mobility rather than group mobility and thus the political management of the system was bound to involve the sorting out of competing claims from different sectors (of which labour became one along with professional associations, corporate business, religion and voluntary associations). Early attempts at socialist or other class-based parties failed because most Americans did not see politics in terms of aggregates of role situations but as the sorting out of problems which arose from their *varied* roles; the Democratic or Republican party may represent different emphases upon role problems to different people. Thus labour unions could see either of the political parties as representing labour demands while members of these unions might see the alternative party as representing what for them might be more fundamental role problems—race, or consumer behaviour or religion. Only with the emergence of Black Power does it seem that one section of the American population has come to see all the other role situations as being reducible to collective mobility. At the same time, as the development of right-wing movements has shown, another section sees all issues as being reducible to the maintenance of order while upholding the values of individual mobility. Whether this heralds a radical reorganization of American politics is hard to say, but it is clear that the Negro movement is galvanized by a corporate demand for upward mobility while the Wallace reaction is based on a fear of symbolic and occupational downward individual mobility.

The consequences of mobility in other countries can be deduced with the same form of analysis. As long as affluent workers in Britain or Germany see themselves simply gaining extra rewards from the system there is unlikely to be change. (There may be alternations between political parties but probably for reasons un-connected with mobility.) The major consequences for political ideologies may be that political choice will be based less on role aggregates than on private interpretations of party programmes, though there is little evidence of this yet. Thus the consciousness of individual mobility or lack of it may come to have precedence over the sense of corporate class. But this assumes a free market in votes and as the United States now shows this is an incorrect assumption. With the particular forms of ethnic, religious, class and national identities that exist in Europe, it is likely that these will continue to dominate political parties. The transition from class-based politics may be towards a more fragmentary party structure based on con-sensus, class, ethnic origins or nationalism, but at the same time producing a large number of people who refuse to identify with any of them because nothing that they say or do has much direct relevance to their particular role situations.

In most industrial countries the politics of students would seem to demonstrate this latter tendency. Student unrest has two dimen-sions: it attacks the inconsistencies of values manifested in national political policies (and these are usually most clearly demonstrated by foreign policy issues), and at the same time it works to change the normative situations in which students live by attacking the management of the universities themselves. But although this has nuisance-value for the political and educational systems it hardly affects the direction of politics. The students have a rapid turnover of members and no power base; the politicians can always respond by closing the universities. The importance of the students is that they show the possibility of action being directed against the politi-cal system without itself generating any political alternative. This is precisely what the American labour unions have been doing for decades, with a more established power base but faced with both the centralization of power and the multiplicity of role situations. As long as the differentiation of roles persists, the concentration of power is likely to persist also. The chances of changing the political system—either in values or structure—is therefore increasingly difficult. The only alternative for dissident groups is to try to create political structures of their own which combine people from several role situations and attempt to operate independently of the system. Such cases are found in tenants movements, civil rights movements, consumer associations, nationalist parties and the like.

In their different ways this is what they do, though some cluster more role situations than others. Their importance is in giving, where the political parties do not, identity to their members. Traditionally this has been done through class struggles, war, civil war and revolution. In industrial countries the struggles may be less violent, but the problems remain. For most people, however, it seems likely that their role situations will not permit them to forge this identity and thus the political system will continue its independent existence. This may bring politics into disrepute (because from each role situation the total political solutions may appear irrelevant, inefficient or absurd) but it will hardly change its course.

However this is in the realm of speculation. For future studies of the relationship between mobility and political change there are two major problems for research. The first of these concerns the relationship between types of mobility and attitude or ideological change; the second the consequences of mobility for the distribution of power. On the first, several recent studies[9] have indicated some of the problems involved, though as Germani's essay suggests (see discussion in Chapter 3) little of this has been systematic nor has it covered many types of situation. These studies however will only produce effective general hypotheses if the cultural context is taken into account as well as the structural. The structural features may well to a great extent explain the cultural, as Chapter 2 tried to specify. Initially, however, a comparative analysis of the attitudes of similar mobile groups should provide the basis from which particular variations in attitudes can be isolated. The variations in turn may be explained by reference to different structural complexes and peculiarities of historical-cultural configurations.

The specifications of attitudes contingent on mobility can, however, only make sense if they are related to the distribution of power. Here the research is much less specific except in so far as attitude changes affect voting patterns. Two issues seem to arise. The first of these relates to the combinations of particular forms of mobility as having a total impact on power. The emergence of the industrial middle class and the decline of the aristocracy in Victorian England provides one example of this. The problem here is probably that of locating the strategic mobile groups. To do this involves the second issue. Assessing the significance of particular forms of mobility for political power requires some conception of the relationship of politics to industrial, religious and other societal factors. One of the difficulties of functionalist models of politics is that power is always the equilibrating feature of society; various interests are harmonized in a structural balancing act. What is more rewarding for research is the conception that political power may rest on certain dominant features of the social structure—the economy or religion or the military or any other combination. Changes in any of these necessarily pose questions for the distribution of power and give rise to different forms of social mobility. To see social mobility as a problem in itself without relating it to changes in social structure is unfruitful. Ultimately *all* mobility is a consequence of changes in the structure and all significant changes in the structure pose questions about the locus of political power. These are the problems towards which future research and analysis should be directed.

Notes
and
References

1/Political Theory and Social Mobility

1 In Book v of *Politics* Aristotle sees the roots of instability and revolution in different societies as lying in changes in the military and economic power of different classes. In Book IV he classifies ranks by socio-political indicators.
2 Edmund Burke, *The Subjection of Women.*
3 Pitrim A. Sorokin, *Social and Cultural Mobility*, Free Press, New York 1959, p. 484.
4 M. Abrams and R. Rose, *Must Labour Lose?* Penguin Books, Harmondsworth, Middlesex 1960.
5 See discussion in Ch. 4 below.
6 For an interpretation along these lines see Robert A. Nisbet, *The Sociological Tradition*, Routledge and Kegan Paul, London 1967.
7 A. de Tocqueville, *Democracy in America*, Doubleday, Garden City, N.Y. 1955, p. 298.
8 Ibid., p. 314.
9 Ibid., p. 585.
10 An argument cogently presented in C. B. MacPherson, *The Political Theory of Possessive Individualism*, Oxford University Press, London 1962.
11 Karl Marx, *Selected Writings in Sociology and Social Philosophy*, edited and introduced by T. B. Bottomore and M. Rubel, Penguin Books, Harmondsworth, Middlesex 1963, p. 233.
12 Ibid., p. 224.
13 Ibid., p. 208.
14 Ibid., pp. 195–6.
15 Ibid., p. 177.
16 This argument is fully explored by Henri Lefebvre, *The Sociology of Marx*, Allen Lane, The Penguin Press, London 1968, Ch. 5.
17 K. Marx, "The Eighteenth Brumaire of Louis Napoleon" in Marx and F. Engels, *Selected Works*, Foreign Languages Publishing House, Moscow 1950, p. 303.
18 H. Gerth and C. W. Mills (eds), *From Max Weber*, Routledge and Kegan Paul, London 1948, p. 186.
19 J. L. Talmon, *Romanticism and Revolt: Europe 1815–1848*, Thames and Hudson, London 1967, p. 21.
20 But see R. Bendix, *Max Weber, an Intellectual Portrait*, Heinemann, London 1960; R. Aron, *Main Currents in Sociological Theory*, Vol. 2, Weidenfeld and Nicolson, London 1967; and Julien Freund, *The Sociology of Max Weber*, Allen Lane, The Penguin Press, London 1968.
21 Bendix, op. cit., p. 103.
22 M. Weber, *The Protestant Ethic and the Spirit of Capitalism*, Allen and Unwin, London 1930, pp. 181–182.
23 Ibid., p. 182.

24 A. de Tocqueville, *The Old Regime and the French Revolution*, Doubleday, Garden City, N.Y. 1955, pp. 176–7.
25 E. Durkheim, *Moral Education: A Study in the Theory and Application of the Sociology of Education*, Free Press, New York 1961, p. 40.
26 E. Durkheim, *Socialism and Saint Simon*, Routledge and Kegan Paul, London 1959, p. 200.
27 E. Durkheim, *Suicide*, Free Press, New York 1951, p. 256.
28 E. Durkheim, *Division of Labour in Society*, Free Press, New York 1947, p. 372.
29 de Tocqueville, *Democracy in America*, II op. cit., p. 302.
30 Ibid., p. 266.
31 'The reverse of what takes place in aristocratic ages then occurs: the men who enter the army are no longer of the highest but of the lowest class.' Ibid., p. 266.
32 Gerth and Mills, op. cit., p. 96.
33 Ibid., p. 87.
34 Ibid., p. 110.
35 R. Michels, *Political Parties*, Collier Books, New York 1962, p. 870.
36 Ibid., p. 191.
37 Ibid., p. 370.
38 For a discussion of Pareto see T. B. Bottomore, *Elites and Society*, Watts, London 1964, especially Chapters I and III, and V. Pareto, *Sociological Writings*, edited by S. E. Finer and translated by Derick Mirfin, Pall Mall Press, London 1966, especially the introduction by Finer.

2/Political Systems and Social Stratification

1 E. Durkheim, *Division of Labour*, op. cit., and *Suicide*, op. cit.
2 The clearest and fullest exposition of Durkheim's and Weber's contribution here is T. Parsons, *The Structure of Social Action*, Free Press, New York 1938.
3 For a discussion see J. P. Nettl, *Political Mobilization*, op. cit., pp. 26–7.
4 W. Goldschmidt, *Comparative Functionalism*, University of California Press, Berkeley 1966.
5 Ibid., p. 132.
6 A. Etzioni, *The Active Society*, Free Press, New York 1968, Part I.
7 T. Parsons, *The Social System*, Free Press, New York 1951.
   E. Evans-Pritchard, *The Nuer*, Oxford University Press, London 1940.
8 Leslie White, *The Evolution of Culture*; M. Sahlins and E. Service, *Culture and Evolution*, University of Michigan Press, Ann Arbor 1962.
9 For examples see S. N. Eisenstadt, *The Political Systems of Empires*, Free Press, New York 1963; Robert M. Marsh, *Comparative Sociology*, Harcourt, Brace and World, New York 1967; G. A. Almond and C. Bingham Powell, *Comparative Politics: A Developmental Approach*, Boston 1966; R. L. Merritt and S. Rokkan, *Comparing Nations*, Yale University Press, New Haven 1966; and Stein Rokkan, *Comparative Research Across Cultures and Nations*, Mouton et Cie, Paris 1968.
10 Neil J. Smelser, "Mechanics of Change and Adjustments to Change", in B. F. Hoselitz and W. E. Moore (eds), *Industrialization and Society*, UNESCO, Paris 1963, pp. 49–74.
11 Neil J. Smelser, *Social Change in the Industrial Revolution*, Routledge and Kegan Paul, London 1959.

12 "Introduction" to G. A. Almond and J. S. Coleman (eds), *The Politics of the Developing Areas*, Princeton University Press, Princeton, N.J. 1960, p. 18.

13 See, for example, S. M. Lipset and R. Bendix, *Social Mobility in Industrial Society*, Heinemann, London 1959.

14 S. N. Eisenstadt, *Modernization—Protest and Change*, Prentice-Hall, Englewood Cliffs, N.J. 1966, p. 7.

15 Karl, W. Deutsch, "Social Mobilization and Political Development", *American Political Science Review*, LV, 3, 1961, pp. 493–514.

16 Eisenstadt, op. cit., p. 146.

17 Eisenstadt, *Political Systems of Empires*, op. cit.

18 See M. Weber, *The Religion of China*, Free Press, New York 1951 and H. Gerth and C. W. Mills (eds), *From Max Weber*, op. cit., Ch. 17.

19 K. Wittfogel, *Oriental Despotism*, Yale University Press, New Haven 1957, p. 3.

20 Ibid., p. 446.

21 Ibid., p. 440.

22 Barrington Moore, Jr., *Social Origins of Dictatorship and Democracy*, Allen Lane, The Penguin Press, London 1966.

23 Ibid., p. 170.

24 Ibid., p. 227.

25 Ibid., p. 169.

3/Mobility and Social and Political Consequences

1 Gino Germani, "Social and Political Consequences of Mobility", in Neil J. Smelser and S. M. Lipset (eds), *Social Structure and Mobility in Economic Development*, Routledge and Kegan Paul, London 1966, pp. 364–94.

2 See S. M. Lipset and R. Bendix, *Social Mobility*, op. cit., and S. M. Miller, "Comparative Social Mobility", *Current Sociology*, 9, 1960, for general surveys of the literature largely in these terms.

3 One of the most convincing recent expositions of the methodological problem involved is Otis Dudley Duncan, "Methodological Issues in the Analysis of Social Mobility", in Neil J. Smelser and S. M. Lipset (eds), op. cit., pp. 51–97. A classic of sociological enquiry based in part on this analysis is Peter M. Blau and Otis Dudley Duncan, *The American Occupational Structure*, John Wiley, New York 1967.

4 Germani, op. cit., p. 366.

5 See note 2 to Ch. 4.

6 Robert K. Merton, *Social Theory and Social Structure*, Free Press, New York 1957, pp. 262–80.

7 For a case study of theoretical exposition of this concept see W. G. Runciman, *Relative Deprivation and Social Justice*, Routledge and Kegan Paul, London 1966.

8 David McClelland, *The Achieving Society*, John Wiley, New York 1961.

9 Ralph Turner, "Modes of Social Ascent through Education: Sponsored and Contest Mobility", in A. H. Halsey, Jean Floud and C. A. Anderson (eds), *Education, Economy and Society*, Free Press, New York 1961, pp. 121–39, and Daniel Lerner, *The Passing of Traditional Society*, University of Chicago Press, Chicago 1958.

4/Mobilization, Mobility and Political Development

1 See especially Gino Germani, "Social Change and Inter-group Conflict", in I. L. Horowitz (ed.), *The New Sociology*, Oxford University Press, New

York 1964; and A. Touraine, "Movilidad social, relaciones de clase y nacionalismo en America Latina", *America Latina*, Vol. 8, No. 1, January/March 1965.

2   Germani, ibid., p. 394.

3   Ibid., p. 396.

4   Ibid., p. 400.

5   D. Bell, *The End of Ideology*, Collier Books, New York 1961, pp. 211–66.

6   B. Russell, *Why I am Not a Christian*, Allen and Unwin, London 1957.

7   For an important analysis of this problem in the Middle East see Daniel Lerner, *The Passing of Traditional Society*, The Free Press, New York 1958.

8   The most lucid exposition of the study of millenialism is Peter Worsley's introduction to his case study, *The Trumpet Shall Sound*, MacGibbon and Kee, London 1968, but see also Yonina Talmon, "The Pursuit of the Millenium", *European Journal of Sociology*, 1963; E. W. Hobsbawm, *Primitive Rebels*, Manchester University Press, Manchester 1959; and V. Lanternari, *The Religions of the Oppressed*, MacGibbon and Kee, London 1963.

9   For a summary see Gwyn Williams, *Artisans and Sans Coulottes*, London.

10 For discussions of these issues see the two volumes edited by Claudio Veliz, *Obstacles to Change in Latin America*, Oxford University Press, London 1965, and *The Politics of Conformity*, Oxford University Press, London 1966.

11 For a discussion of the thesis of labour commitment see W. E. Moore and A. S. Feldman, *Labor Commitment and Social Change*, Social Science Research Council, New York 1960.

12 P. Gonzalez Casanova, "L'évolution du systeme des classes en Mexique" *Cahiers Internationaux de Sociologie*, Vol. 12, No. 39, 1965, pp. 113–36.

13 O. Lewis, *The Children of Sanchez*, Secker & Warburg, London 1962.

14 A. Touraine, "Industrialization et conscience ouvrière à São Paulo", *Sociologie du Travail*, Vol. 3, No. 41 (1961), pp. 77–95.

15 See, e.g. Octavio Ianni, "Condicoes instituconais do comparamento politico operario", *Revista Brasiliense*, No. 36, 1961, pp. 16–39.

16 Azis Simão, "Industrialisme et syndicalisme en Bresil", *Sociologie du Travail*, Vol. 3, No. 4, 1961, pp. 378–88; Michel Lowry and Sarah Chucid, "Opinoes et atitudes de lideres sindicais metaluricos", *Revista Brasiliera ed Estudos Politicos* (Belo Horizonte), No. 13, Jan. 1962, pp. 132–69.

17 H. Lansberger, "The Labour Elite: Is It Revolutionary?", in S. M. Lipset and A. Solari, *Elites in Latin America*, Oxford University Press, London 1966.

18 Robert Payne, *Labor and Politics in Peru*, Yale University Press, New Haven 1965.

19 F. Fanon, *The Wretched of the Earth*, MacGibbon and Kee, London 1965, p. 98.

20 See discussion in I. Davies, *African Trade Unions*, Penguin Books, Harmondsworth, Middlesex 1966.

21 Bottomore and Rubel, op. cit., p. 147.

22 Ibid., p. 207.

23 Ibid., p. 170.

24 See E. Durkheim, *Division of Labour*, op. cit., especially chapters 2, 3, 6. For a persuasive critique see Percy Cohen, *Modern Social Theory*, Heinemann, London 1967, pp. 224–34.

25 C. Wagley, *An Introduction to Brazil*, University of Chicago Press, Chicago 1962, p. 126.

5/Mobility and Politics in Industrial Society

1 Ralph Dahrendorf, *Class and Class Conflict in Industrial Society*, Routledge and Kegan Paul, London 1959.

2 See G. Lenski, "Status Crystallization: A non-vertical Dimension of Social Status", *American Sociological Review*, 19, 1954, pp. 405–13; W. S. Landekker, "Class Boundaries", *American Sociological Review*, 25, 1960, 868–77; Johan Galtung, "International Relations and International Conflicts: A Sociological Approach", *Transactions of the Sixth World Congress of Sociology*, 1966, Vol. 1, pp. 121–61; and "Rank and Social Integration: A multidimensional approach", in B. Berger, M. Zelditch and B. Anderson (eds), *Sociological Theories in Progress*, Vol. 1, Houghton and Mifflin, Boston 1966.

3 For a discussion of the relationship between structure and systems see D. Lockwood, "Social Integration and System Integration", in G. K. Zollschan and W. Hirsh (eds), *Exploration in Social Change*, Routledge and Kegan Paul, London 1964, 244–56, and P. Cohen, *Modern Social Theory*, Heinemann, London 1968, Ch. 6.

4 See R. K. Merton, *Social Theory and Social Structure*, Free Press, New York 1957, Ch. 8 and and 9, and W. G. Runciman, *Relative Deprivation and Social Justice*, Routledge and Kegan Paul, London 1966.

5 Edmund Leach, "Liberty, Equality, Fraternity", *New Statesman*, July 8, 1966, pp. 55–6.

6 A. Tannenbaum, *The True Society*, Jonathan Cape, London 1964, p. 141.

7 D. Bell, *The End of Ideology*, Collier-Macmillan, New York 1961, p. 218.

8 See essays by R. Alford, R. McKenzie and R. Silver, M. Doggan and J. Linz in S. M. Lipset and S. Rokkan (eds), *Party Systems and Voter Alignments*, Free Press, New York 1967, for some European and North American comparisons.

9 e.g. Abrams and Rose, op. cit.

10 Lipset and Rokkan, op. cit., p. 21.

11 R. Blauner, *Alienation and Freedom*, University of Chicago Press, Chicago 1964.

12 A. Touraine, *L'Evolution du travail ouvrier aux usines Renault*, CNRS, Paris 1955.

13 See S. Mallet, *La nouvelle classe ouvrière*. Editions du Seuil, Paris 1963, who uses technological organizational variables in a way not dissimilar to those developed by Blauner.

14 "The Inter-industry Propensity to Strike", in R. Kornhauser, A. Dubin and A. Ross, *Industrial Conflict*, McGraw-Hill, New York 1954, pp. 189–212.

15 D. Lockwood, J. H. Goldthorpe, F. Bechoffer and J. Platt, "The Affluent Worker and the Thesis of Embourgeoisement", *Sociology*, Vol. 1, No. 1, 1967, p. 24. For a full report of the survey see Goldthorpe, Lockwood, Bechoffer and Platt, *The Affluent Worker*, 4 volumes, Cambridge University Press, Cambridge 1968–69.

16 Franklin Frazier, *Black Bourgeoisie*, Collier Books, New York 1962, p. 195.

17 I. U. Esien-Udom, *Black Nationalism*, Penguin Books, Harmondsworth, Middlesex 1962.

18 S. M. Lipset, "The Sources of the Radical Right", in D. Bell (ed.), *The Radical Right*, Doubleday, Garden City, N.Y. 1964, p. 326.

19 S. M. Lipset, "The New American Right", *New Society*, October 8, 1968, 477–9.

20 T. Parson, "Social Strains in America", in D. Bell (ed.), op. cit.

120/*Notes and References*

21 See, e.g., Milton Freedman, *Capitalism and Freedom*, University of Chicago Press, Chicago 1962.
22 See H. Lefebvre, op. cit., Ch. 5 for a critique and for Trotsky see his *The Revolution Betrayed*, Russell and Russell, New York 1937.
23 The classic exposition is James Burnham, *The Managerial Revolution*, John Day, New York 1941. Its relevance to British politics is the major theme of C. A. R. Crosland, *The Future of Socialism*, Jonathan Cape, London 1956.
24 See W. L. Guttsman, *The British Political Elite*, MacGibbon and Kee, London 1963, especially Chapters 8, 9, 10 for account of the part played by political societies in British politics.
25 See summary in Jean Blondel, *Voters, Parties and Leaders*, Penguin Books, Harmondsworth, Middlesex 1963.
26 The American literature on this is extensive, but see R. E. Dahl, *Who Governs?* Yale University Press, New Haven 1961, for a good example.
27 See George K. Schueller, "The Politburo", in H. D. Lasswell and D. Lerner (eds), *World Revolutionary Elites*, The M.I.T. Press, Cambridge, Mass. 1966, pp. 97–178.
28 Milovan Djilas, *The New Class*, Thames and Hudson, London 1957.

6/Differentiation and Political Power

1 P. Cohen, op. cit., Chapters 6 and 8.
2 A. Gouldner, "Reciprocity and Autonomy in functional Theory", in Llewellyn L. Gross (ed.), *Symposium on Sociological Theory*, Harper & Row, Evanston, Ill. 1959.
3 L. Trotsky, *The Revolution Betrayed*, Pioneer Publishers, New York 1945.
4 The most useful critical accounts in English of Gramsci's work are John Merrington, "Theory and Practice in Gramsci's Marxism", *Socialist Register*, Merlin Press, London 1968, pp. 145–76 and Gwyn Williams, "Gramsci's Concept of 'Egemonia' ", *Journal of the History of Ideas*, Vol. XXI, 4, 1960, p. 586 ff. To date the major translation of Gramsci's work is *The Modern Prince*, Lawrence and Wishart, London 1958.
5 D. Easton, *The Political System*, Knopf, New York 1953.
6 A. Stinchcombe, "Agricultural Enterprise and Rural Class Relations", in R. Bendix and S. M. Lipset (eds), *Class, Status and Power*, Routledge and Kegan Paul, London 1966, pp. 182–90.
7 A. Touraine, "Movilidad social, relaciones de clase y nacionalismo en America Latina", *America Latina*, Vol. 8, 1965.
8 Quoted in Okoi Arikpo, *The Devolopment of Modern Nigeria*, Penguin Books, Harmondsworth, Middlesex 1967, p. 155.
9 Some of the relevant work on European cases is found in Richard F. Hamilton, *Affluence and the French Worker: The Fourth Republic Experience*, Princeton University Press, Princeton 1967; S. Mallet, *La Nouvelle Classe Ouvrière*, op. cit.; and Goldthorpe, Lockwood et al., *The Affluent Worker*, op. cit.; on the United States, R. Blauner, *Alienation and Freedom*, op. cit.; on developing countries, Maurice Zeitlin, *Revolutionary Politics and the Cuban Working Class*, Princeton University Press, Princeton 1967; M. Tumin, *Class and Social Change in Puerto Rico*, Princeton University Press, Princeton 1961; and P. C. Lloyd (ed.), *New Elites of Tropical Africa*, Oxford University Press, London 1966. Some of the wider issues concerning the correlation of stratification and voting patterns in Western Europe, North America and Australia are covered in S. M. Lipset and S. Rokkan (eds), op. cit.

Bibliography

Select Bibliography and Suggestions for Further Reading

(Where the publisher of the title is not named here, full details will be found in the 'Works Cited' section.)

There is no basic introductory text to the topic nor any comprehensive collection of data. However, three books provide among them important indications of the range of problems involved. Pitrim A. Sorokin's, *Social and Cultural Mobility*, is a selection from the author's two major works, *Social and Cultural Dynamics* and *Social Mobility*. Although some of the evidence has been surpassed by more recent research, few of the observations and theories have dated. N. J. Smelser and S. M. Lipset's *Social Structure and Mobility in Economic Development*, includes some outstanding papers on problems of contemporary societies, concentrating on less prosperous countries. R. Bendix and S. M. Lipset's, *Class, Status and Power*, is the *sine qua non* for the study of social stratification. Although this book does not explore social mobility in any great detail its many papers on aspects of the relationship between class and politics make it an indispensible source book.

Beyond these general introductions the study can proceed in several directions. For the genesis of ideas on social mobility itself there is no satisfactory introduction and the reader is advised to consult the basic texts, notably those by Marx, Weber, Durkheim, de Tocqueville, Pareto, Mosca. T. B. Bottomore's, *Elites and Society*, provides a good summary of some aspects of the study while some of the better surveys of the origins of sociology deal with the subject in the course of the presentation of more general material. Of these Raymond Aron's two-volume study, *Main Currents in Sociological Theory*, and Robert A. Nisbett's, *The Sociological Tradition*, are probably the most useful. Bottomore's *Classes in Modern Society*, (Allen and Unwin, London 1965) is a useful introduction to some of the basic issues in the origins and subsequent development of sociological theories of social stratification, as is Dahrendorf's *Class and Class Conflict in Industrial Society*.

On the sociological analysis of social mobility in contemporary industrial societies, S. M. Lipset and R. A. Bendix, *Social Mobility in Industrial Society*, is the basic text. Some of the conclusions of this study have, however, been contested on methodological grounds, but the main issues are discussed by Otis Dudley Duncan, Harold L. Wilensky and Natalie Rogoff Romsoy in Smelser and Lipset. Peter M. Blau and Otis Dudley Duncan's *The American Occupational Structure*, is one of the most systematic studies of occupational mobility. Some of the major issues of social mobility have in fact been studied in the context of educational opportunities. A. H. Halsey, Jean Floud and C. Arnold Anderson's *Education, Economy and Society*, collects a number of essays published in the 1950s, while James C. Coleman's *Equality of Educational Opportunity*, (Department of Health, Education and Welfare, Washington 1966) is the most sophisticated methodological analysis of the problem in any one country.

Andre Beteille's *Social Inequality*, (Penguin Books, Harmondsworth, Middlesex 1969) is primarily a collection of important essays on stratification in pre-industrial and transitional societies. Chapter 5 of Robert M. Marsh, *Comparative Sociology*, attempts to summarize the major findings of research in stratification and mobility.

In developing countries the study of mobility has either concentrated on the recruitment of élites or on the wider questions of mobilization. On élites two collections of essays provide a general survey: S. M. Lipset and Aldo Solari (eds), *Elites in Latin America*, and on mobilization an important attempt at synthesis is J. P. Nettl's *Political Mobilization*, while some of the general issues are discussed in the essays by Germani, Touraine and Deutsch listed in the bibliography of works cited. Germani's *Politica y sociedad en una epoca de transicion*, (Buenos Aires 1963) is the classic exposition of the mobilization thesis in a Latin American context, while Moore and Feldman, Daniel Lerner and Davies raise related questions in other societal contexts. Some of the basic issues of industrialization are raised in Tom Burns (ed.), *Industrial Man*, (Penguin Books, Harmondsworth, Middlesex 1969).

The relationship between social mobility and political change is studied explicitly for Great Britain in W. G. Runciman's *Relative Deprivation and Social Justice*, and in Vol. 2 of D. Lockwood et al., *The Affluent Worker*. There are a large number of similar studies of the United States, but Robert Blauner, *Alienation and Freedom*, summarizes much of the literature, though from the perspective of types of technology. David Apter's *The Politics of Modernization*, attempts to relate political change to changes at all social levels in the developing countries, while Frantz Fanon's *The Wretched Earth*, sees mobility as a device by the foreign-dominated urban élites to perpetuate a *status quo* to the disadvantage of the rural populations. Cyril E. Black (ed.), *The Transformation of Russian Society*, (Harvard University Press, Cambridge, Mass. 1960) includes a number of important essays on the relationship between changes in social stratification and political control in Tsarist and Soviet Russia.

There are several books and essays which try to provide frameworks within which changes in forms of social stratification and political organization and ideologies might be examined. Neil J. Smelser's "Mechanisms of Change and Adjustments to Change" in Burns is perhaps the most comprehensive approach. S. N. Eisenstadt, *Modernization Process and Change*, Barrington Moore, Jr., *Social Origins of Dictatorship and Democracy*, and J. P. Nettl's *Political Mobilization*, provide three important perspectives, Eisenstadt and Nettl owing much to the writing of Talcott Parsons and Moore to a Marxist histographic tradition.

Issues of cultural mobility and the relationship between mobility and changes in ideologies and beliefs owe much to the writings of Max Weber, notably his *Protestant Ethic and the Spirit of Capitalism*. Of the subsequent debate on the relationship between social and ideological change, much of the literature does not bear directly on the subject of this study though K. Mannheim, *Ideology and Utopia* (Routledge and Kegan Paul, London 1936) and P. Berger, Thomas Luckmann, *The Social Construction of Reality*, (Allen Lane, The Penguin Press, London 1967) are important general approaches to the problem. Luckmann and Berger's "Social Mobility and Personal Identity", *European Journal of Sociology*, v, 1964, p. 331 ff., is an attempt to raise a number of questions about the effects of mobility for the construction of ideologies in the United States and Western Europe. For developing countries there is a considerable literature on changes in attitudes which accompany shifts in stratification, some of which is summarized and discussed in the essays by Bendix, Crockett, Seligman and Germani in Smelser and Lipset. J. P. Nettl is a general consideration of the context and texture of these issues in a political framework.

There are no satisfactory books which use changes in social stratification as the basis for a general theory of political change. Observations such as de Tocqueville's and Durkheim's have hardly produced serious attempts at generalization. For the past half-century the main problems have been the refinement of definitions of mobility and the improvement of the tools of analysis. Political scientists tend also to have been disinterested in social stratification and sociologists disinterested in political change. This is therefore the only contemporary book which attempts to bring these two sets of problems together. However, an important book by a political philosopher which deals in part with the politics of social differences is Brian Barry, *Political Argument*, (Routledge and Kegan Paul, London 1967). Unfortunately there is no treatment of social mobility as such.

Works Cited

ABRAMS, M. and ROSE, R., *Must Labour Lose?*, Penguin Books, Harmondsworth, Middlesex 1960.
ALMOND, GABRIEL A. and COLEMAN, JAMES S. (eds), *The Politics of the Developing Areas*, Princeton University Press, Princeton 1960.
ALMOND, GABRIEL A. and BINGHAM POWELL, C. (eds), *Comparative Politics: A Developmental Approach*, Little, Brown, Boston 1966.
APTER, DAVID, *The Politics of Modernization*, University of Chicago Press, Chicago 1965.
ARIKPO, OKOI, *The Development of Modern Nigeria*, Penguin Books, Harmondsworth, Middlesex 1967.
ARISTOTLE, *Politics*.
ARON, RAYMOND, *Main Currents in Sociological Theory*, 2 vols., Weidenfeld and Nicolson, London 1965, 1967.
BELL, DANIEL, *The End of Ideology*, Collier-Macmillan, New York 1961.
BENDIX, R., *Max Weber, an Intellectual Portrait*, Heinemann, London 1960.
BENDIX, R. and LIPSET, S. M. (eds), *Class, Status and Power*, Routledge and Kegan Paul, London 1966.
BLAU, PETER M. and DUNCAN, OTIS DUDLEY, *The American Occupational Structure*, John Wiley, New York 1967.
BLAUNER, ROBERT, *Alienation and Freedom*, University of Chicago Press, Chicago 1964.

BLONDEL, JEAN, *Voters, Parties and Leaders*, Penguin Books, Harmondsworth, Middlesex 1963.

BOTTOMORE, T. B., *Elites and Society*, Watts and Co., London 1964.

BURKE, EDMUND, *Subjection of Women*.

BURNHAM, JAMES, *The Managerial Revolution*, Penguin Books, Harmondsworth, Middlesex 1941.

CASANOVA, P. GONZALEZ, "L'évolution du systeme des classes en Mexique", *Cahiers Internationaux de Sociologie*, Vol. 12, No. 39, 1965, 113–36.

COHEN, PERCY, *Modern Social Theory*, Heinemann, London 1968.

CROSLAND, C. A. R., *The Future of Socialism*, Jonathan Cape, London 1956.

DAHL, ROBERT E., *Who Governs?*, Yale University Press, New Haven 1961.

DAHRENDORF, RALPH, *Class And Class Conflict in Industrial Society*, Routledge and Kegan Paul, London 1959.

DAVIES, IOAN, *African Trade Unions*, Penguin Books, Harmondsworth, Middlesex 1966.

DEUTSCH, KARL W., "Social Mobilization and Political Development", *American Political Science Review*, lv, 3, 1961, 493–514.

DJILAS, MILOVAN, *The New Class*, Thames and Hudson, London 1957.

DURKHEIM, EMILE, *Division of Labour in Society*, Free Press, Glencoe, Ill. 1947.

—— *Moral Education: A Study in the Theory and Application of the Sociology of Education*, Free Press, New York 1961.

—— *Socialism and Saint Simon*, Routledge and Kegan Paul, London 1959.

—— *Suicide*, Routledge and Kegan Paul, London 1952.

EASTON, DAVID, *The Political System*, Knopf, New York 1953.

EISENSTADT, S. N., *Modernization—Protest and Change*, Prentice-Hall, Englewood-Cliffs, N.J. 1966.

—— *Political Systems of Empire*, The Free Press, New York 1963.

ESIEN-UDOM, E., *Black Nationalism*, Penguin Books, Harmondsworth, Middlesex 1962.

ETZIONI, AMITAI, *The Active Society*, The Free Press, New York 1968.

FANON, FRANTZ, *The Wretched of the Earth*, MacGibbon and Kee, London 1965.

FRAZIER, E. FRANKLIN, *Black Bourgeoisie*, Collier Books, New York, 1962.

FREEDMAN, MILTON, *Capitalism and Freedom*, University of Chicago Press, Chicago 1962.

FREUND, JULIEN, *The Sociology of Max Weber*, Allen Lane, The Penguin Press, London 1968.

GALTUNG, JOHAN, "International Relations and International Conflicts: a Sociological Approach", *Transactions of the Sixth World Congress of Sociology*, 1966, Vol. I, 121–161.

—— "Rank and Social Integration: a Multidimensional Approach", in B. Berger, M. Zelditch and B. Anderson (eds), *Sociological Theories in Progress*, Vol. I, Houghton and Mifflin, Boston 1966.

GERMANI, GINO, "Social Change and Inter-Group Conflict", in I. L. Horowitz (ed.), *The New Sociology*, New York 1964.

—— "Social and Political Consequences of Mobility", in N. J. Smelser and S. M. Lipset (*q.v.*).

GERTH, H. and MILLS, C. WRIGHT (eds), *From Max Weber*, Oxford University Press, New York 1946.

GOLDSCHMIDT, WALTER, *Comparative Functionalism*, University of California Press, Berkeley 1966.

GOULDNER, ALVIN W., "Reciprocity and Autonomy in Functional Theory", in Llewellyn L. Gross (ed.), *Symposium on Sociological Theory*, Harper and Row, New York 1959.

GRAMSCI, ANTONIO, *The Modern Prince*, Lawrence and Wishart, London 1958.

GUTTSMAN, W. L., *The British Political Elite*, MacGibbon and Kee, London 1963.

HALSEY, A. H., FLOUD, J. and ANDERSON, C. ARNOLD (eds), *Education, Economy and Society*, The Free Press, New York, 1961.

HAMILTON, RICHARD F., *Affluence and the French Worker: the Fourth Republic Experience*, Princeton University Press, Princeton 1967.

HOBSBAWM, E. J., *Primitive Rebels*, University of Manchester Press, Manchester 1959.

IANNI, OCTAVIO, "Condicoes instituconais do comparamento politico operario", *Revista Brasilinese*, 36, 1961, pp. 16–39.

KORNHAUSER, R., DUBIN, A. and ROSS, A., *Industrial Conflict*, McGraw-Hill, New York 1956.

LANDEKKER, WERNER S., "Class Boundaries", *American Sociological Review*, 25, 1960, pp. 868–77.

LANSBERGER, H., "The Labor Elite: Is It Revolutionary?" in S. M. Lipset and A. Solari (eds), *Elites in Latin America*, Oxford University Press, New York 1966.

LANTERNARI, VITTORIO, *The Religion of the Oppressed*, MacGibbon and Kee, London 1963.

LEACH, EDMUND, "Liberty, Equality, Fraternity", *New Statesman*, July 8, 1966, pp. 55–6.

LEFEBVRE, HENRI, *The Sociology of Marx*, Allen Lane, The Penguin Press, London 1968.

LENSKI, GERHARDT, "Status Crystallization: a non-Vertical Dimension of Social Status", *American Sociological Review*, 19, 1954, pp. 405–13.

LERNER, DANIEL, *The Passing of Traditional Society*, University of Chicago Press, Chicago 1958.

LEWIS, OSCAR, *The Children of Sanchez*, Secker and Warburg, London 1962.

LIPSET, S. M., "The New American Right", *New Society*, October 8, 1968, pp. 477–9.

——— "The Sources of the Radical Right", in D. Bell (ed.), *The Radical Right*, Doubleday, Garden City, N.Y. 1964.

LIPSET, S. M. and BENDIX, R., *Social Mobility in Industrial Society*, Heinemann, London 1959.

LIPSET, S. M. and ROKKAN S. (eds), *Party Systems and Voter Alignments*, Free Press, New York 1967.

LLOYD, P. C. (ed.), *New Elites of Tropical Africa*, Oxford University Press, London 1966.

LOCKWOOD, DAVID, "Social Integration and System Integration", in G. K. Zollschan and W. Hirsh (eds), *Explorations in Social Change*, Routledge and Kegan Paul, London 1964, pp. 244–56.

LOCKWOOD, D., GOLDTHORPE, J. H., BECHHOFER, F. and PLATT, J., "The Affluent Worker and the Thesis of Embourgeoisement", *Sociology*, 1, 1, 1967.

LOCKWOOD, D., GOLDTHORPE, J. H., BECHHOFER, F. and PLATT J., *The Affluent Worker*, 4 vols., Cambridge University Press, Cambridge 1965–70.

LOWRY, MICHEL and CHUCID, SARAH, "Opinoes et atitudes de lideres sindicais metaluricos", *Revista Brasiliera ed estudes Politicos*, (Bel Horizonte), No. 13, January 1962, pp. 132–69.

MCCLELLAND, DAVID C., *The Achieving Society*, John Wiley, New York 1961.

MACPHERSON, C. B., *Political Theory of Possessive Individualism*, Oxford University Press, Oxford 1962.

MALLET, SERGE, *La nouvelle classe ouvrière*, Editious du Seuil, Paris 1963.

MARSH, ROBERT N., *Comparative Sociology*, Harcourt, Brace and World, New York 1967.

MARX, KARL, "The Eighteenth Brumaire of Louis Napoleon", in K. Marx and F. Engels, *Selected Works*, Foreign Language Publishing House, Moscow 1950.

—— *Selected Writings in Sociology and Social Philosophy*, edited and introduced by T. B. Bottomore and M. Rubel, Penguin Books, Harmondsworth, Middlesex 1963.

MERRINGTON, JOHN, "Theory and Practice in Gramsci's Marxism", *Socialist Register*, Merlin Press, London 1968.

MERRITT, R. L. and ROKKAN, S., (eds), *Comparing Nations*, Yale University Press, New Haven 1966.

MERTON, ROBERT K., *Social Theory and Social Structure*, The Free Press, New York 1957.

MICHELS, ROBERT, *Political Parties*, Collier Books, New York 1962.

MILLER, S. M., "Comparative Social Mobility", *Current Sociology*, 9, 1960.

MOORE, BARRINGTON, Jr., *Social Origins of Dictatorship and Democracy*, Allen Lane, The Penguin Press, London 1966.

MOORE, WILBERT S. and FELDMAN, ARNOLD S. (eds), *Labor Commitment and Social Change*, Social Science Research Council, New York 1960.

NETTL, J. P., *Political Mobilization*, Faber and Faber, London 1966.

NISBET, ROBERT A., *The Sociological Tradition*, Routledge and Kegan Paul, London 1967.

PARETO, VILFREDO, *Sociological Writings*, edited with an introduction by S. E. Finer, translated by Derick Mirfin, Pall Mall Press, London 1966.

PARSONS, TALCOTT, *The Social System*, The Free Press, New York 1951.

—— *The Structure of Social Action*, The Free Press, New York 1938.

PAYNE, ROBERT, *Labor and Politics in Peru*, Yale University Press, New Haven 1965.

ROKKAN, STEIN, *Comparative Research Across Cultures and Nations*, Mouton et Cie, Paris 1968.

RUNCIMAN, W. G., *Relative Deprivation and Social Justice*, Routledge and Kegan Paul, London 1966.

RUSSELL, BERTRAM, *Why I am not a Christian*, Allen and Unwin, London 1958.

SAHLINS, M. and SERVICE, E., *Culture and Evolution*, University of Michigan Press, Ann Arbor, Mich. 1962.

SCHUELLER, GEORGE K., "The Politburo", in H. D. Lasswell and D. Lerner (eds), *World Revolutionary Elites*, The M.I.T. Press, Cambridge, Mass. 1966, pp. 97–178.

SIMÃO, AZIS, "Industrialisme et syndicalisme en Bresil", *Sociologie du Travail*, Vol. 3, No. 4, Paris 1961, pp. 378–88.

SMELSER, NEIL J., "Mechanics of Change and Adjustments to Change", in T. Burns (ed.), *Industrial Man*, Penguin Books, Harmondsworth, Middlesex 1969.

SMELSER, N. J. and LIPSET, S. M., *Social Structure and Mobility in Economic Development*, Routledge and Kegan Paul, London 1966.

SOROKIN, PITRIM A., *Social and Cultural Mobility*, The Free Press, Glencoe, Ill. 1959.

STINCHCOMBE, A. L., "Agricultural Enterprise and Rural Class Relations", in R. Bendix and S. M. Lipset (eds), *q.v.*

TALMON, J. L., *Romanticism and Revolt: Europe 1815–1848*, Thames and Hudson, London 1967.

TALMON, Y., "The Pursuit of the Millenium", *European Journal of Sociology*, 1963.

TANNENBAUM, A., *The True Society*, Jonathan Cape, London 1964.

DE TOCQUEVILLE, A., *Democracy in America*, Doubleday, Garden City, N.Y. 1955.

────── *The Old Regime and the French Revolution*, Doubleday, Garden City, N.Y. 1955.

TOURAINE, A., *L'evolution du travail ouvrièr aux usines Renault*, Paris 1955.

────── "Industrialization et conscience ouvriére a São Paulo", *Sociologie du Travail*, Paris, Vol. 3, No. 4, 1961, pp. 77–95.

────── "Movilidad social, relaciones de clase y nacionalismo en America Latina", *America Latina*, Sao Paulo, Vol. 8, No. 1, January/March 1965.

TROTSKY, LEON, *The Revolution Betrayed*, Pioneer Publishers, New York 1945.

TUMIN, M., *Class and Social Change in Puerto Rico*, Princeton University Press, Princeton 1964.

TURNER, RALPH, "Modes of Social Ascent Through Education: Sponsored and Contest Mobility", in A. H. Halsey, Jean Floud and C. Arnold Anderson, (*q.v.*).

VELIZ, CLAUDIO (ed.), *Obstacles to Change in Latin America*, Oxford University Press, London 1965.

VELIZ, CLAUDIO (ed.), *The Politics of Conformity in Latin America*, Oxford University Press, London 1965.

WAGLEY, CHARLES, *An Introduction to Brazil*, University of Chicago Press, Chicago 1962.

WEBER, MAX, *The Protestant Ethic and the Spirit of Capitalism*, Allen and Unwin, London 1930.

────── *The Religion of China*, The Free Press, New York, 1951.

WHYTE, LESLIE, *The Evolution of Culture*, McGraw-Hill, New York 1959.

WILLIAMS, GWYN, *Artisans and Sans-Coulottes*, Routledge and Kegan Paul, London, 1968.

────── "Gramsci's Concept of 'Egemonia' ", *Journal of the History of Ideas*, XXI, 4, 1960, p. 586 ff.

WITTFOGEL, KARL, *Oriental Despotism*, Yale University Press, New Haven 1957.

WORSLEY, PETER, *The Trumpet Shall Sound*, MacGibbon and Kee, London 1968.

ZEITLIN, MAURICE, *Revolutionary Politics and the Cuban Working Class*, Princeton University Press, Princeton 1967.

Index